一起来说

以图片为基础的课堂交际练习

Learning to Speak

Picture-based Communicative Activities for the Language Classroom

编著： 卢百可　Patrick Lucas
　　　 邓秀均　Xiujun Deng
绘图： 宁卓涛　Zhuotao Ning

北京语言文化大学出版社

(京)新登字 157 号

图书在版编目（CIP）数据

一起来说/（美）卢百可（LUCAS, P.）编；邓秀均编著．
－北京：北京语言文化大学出版社，1998.8
ISBN 7－5619－0630－7

Ⅰ．一…
Ⅱ．①卢… ②邓…
Ⅲ．①英语－口语－训练－英汉 ②对外汉语教学－口语－训练－汉、英
Ⅳ．H319.9

中国版本图书馆 CIP 数据核字（98）第 04308 号
著作权合同登记：01－98－1185 号

责任印制：汪学发
出版发行：北京语言文化大学出版社
　　　　　（北京海淀区学院路 15 号　邮政编码 100083）
印　　刷：北京北林印刷厂
经　　销：全国新华书店
版　　次：1999 年 1 月第 1 版　1999 年 1 月第 1 次印刷
开　　本：850 毫米×1168 毫米　1/16　印张：17.75
字　　数：110 千字　印数：0001－3000
书　　号：ISBN 7－5619－0630－7/H·9803
定　　价：36.00 元

目　录

前言 ……………………………………………………………………（ 1 ）
    1. 本书简介 ……………………………………………………（ 1 ）
    2. 教师对练习的解释和说明 …………………………………（ 2 ）
        分组 ……………………………………………………（ 2 ）
        发言 ……………………………………………………（ 3 ）
        总结练习 ………………………………………………（ 3 ）
        教师在练习中的角色 …………………………………（ 3 ）
        练习的目的和应该使用的语言 ………………………（ 4 ）
    3. 交际法的基本原理 …………………………………………（ 4 ）
        导言和原理 ……………………………………………（ 4 ）
        交际法的实际应用 ……………………………………（ 5 ）
        交际策略 ………………………………………………（ 6 ）
        准确性和偏误 …………………………………………（ 7 ）

练习 ……………………………………………………………………（ 1 ）
    一、描述和排列（一）…………………………………………（ 1 ）
       描述和排列（二）…………………………………………（24）
    二、描述和比较 ………………………………………………（56）
    三、描述和绘画 ………………………………………………（79）
    四、看图说话 …………………………………………………（88）
    五、看图编故事 ………………………………………………（111）
    六、看图议论（一）……………………………………………（124）
       看图议论（二）……………………………………………（130）

后记 ……………………………………………………………………（136）

Table of Contents

PREFACE ··· (9)

   Introduction ·· (9)

   Teacher Explanation and Introduction to the Exercises ··················· (10)
      GROUP WORK ··· (10)
      PRESENTATIONS ··· (11)
      ENDING ACTIVITY ··· (12)
      TEACHER'S ROLE DURING ACTIVITIES ······································· (12)
      WHAT KIND OF LANGUAGE SHOULD THEY USE? ···························· (13)

   Brief Overview of Communicative Language Teaching (CLT) ··········· (13)
      INTRODUCTION AND PRINCIPLES ·· (13)
      SOME PRACTICAL ASPECTS OF CLT ··· (14)
      COMMUNICATIVE STRATEGIES ··· (15)
      ACCURACY AND ERRORS ·· (16)

EXERCISES ·· (2)
      ORDERING PICTURES I & II ·· (2)
      COMPARING PICTURES ··· (57)
      DRAWING A PICTURE ··· (80)
      TELLING A STORY ·· (89)
      CREATING A STORY ·· (112)
      DISCUSSING A TOPIC I & II ·· (125)

Postscript ··· (137)

前　言

1. 本书简介

这本书包括六项以图片为基础的供课堂使用的练习。依据交际法原则(见3.交际法的基本原理),通过各种形式的练习,促使学生在小组中与同伴用目的语谈话和交际,帮助学生有效地学习用外语进行交际。这些有着明确任务和任务终点的练习,既非常有趣,又十分刺激,给学生一定的自主权,将带给学生丰富和具有变化的课堂体验。总之,学生要使用目的语来完成交际任务,就在这个有目的性的、完成任务的过程中,学生也进行了练习和学习。

这些练习适用于各种课型、各种语言水平,以及任何鼓励说话和交际练习的语言教学。学生只需用他们已经掌握了的语言知识,在自己现有的水平上完成练习任务。这些练习除了具有较广泛的内在的交际要素以外,还包括一系列词汇和语法点。从家庭到医院,从公园到公共汽车上,不同的环境和动作要求学生选择不同的句子形式和语言结构。比如:正在进行时态、存在句、方位词、趋向补语等等。除了练习交际的宏观技巧以外,学生还可以在听和说的过程中及时得到宝贵的效果反馈。比如从对方的反应就可以监督自己的发音、语调、语速以及选词造句是否正确。

每项练习既有教师指导的集体活动,比如教师进行举例和总结(占时间较少),又有学生的独立活动,比如分组练习(所占时间较多)。

由于绝大部分练习重在信息差异的比较,如果失去信息的差异,交际也就失去了意义(见3.交际法的基本原理),因此这本书不能直接发给学生,教师应该在使用的时候撕下本次所需的图片,发给学生。

这本书的练习项目如下:

(1)描述和排列(一)、(二),共26个,52页。

每对学生人手一张有成行小图的图片,彼此不能看对方的图片,分别描述和排列每行小图。

(2)描述和比较,共10个,20页。

每对学生人手一张内容相似的图片,彼此不能看对方的图片,分别描述和比较两张图片。

(3)描述和绘画,共12个,6页。

每对学生一人手拿一张图片描述画面内容,另一人不能看对方的图片,只能根据对方的描述和指点把画面内容画出来。

(4)看图说话,共20个,20页。

每组学生手拿一张有一系列情节的图片,共同讨论,根据画面内容讲述一个完整的故事。

(5)看图编故事,共10个,10页。

每组学生手拿一张有连续性情节的但其中有空白画面的图片,共同讨论,根据画面内容编一个完整的故事。

(6)看图议论(一)、(二),共12个,9页。

每组学生手拿一张反映某种社会现象的图片,共同讨论画面内容,并对这种社会现象发表看法。

每项练习都有详细的说明(包括练习目的、使用方法和注意事项)和举例,并且尽可能按照从易到难的顺序安排。

本书的编写参考了一些已出版的教材,像 Yorkey 的 *Talk - A - Tivities* 和 Winn - Bell Olsen 的 *Look Again Pictures* 等等。他们为交际法在课堂教学的应用做出了非常大的贡献,在此谨向他们致以诚挚的谢意。

2. 教师对练习的解释和说明

在进行每项练习前,教师给学生一个很好的练习说明是十分必要的。一个详细的说明可以节省大量的课堂时间,还可以使学生少受挫折。如果没有它,那么每项练习就不会达到预期的目的。不但第一次的说明是十分重要的,而且在以后的练习中简短的说明也是必不可少的。

第一次做每项练习时,教师首先应该使用书中为举例所提供的图片,与学生一起完成练习。每项说明都包括此项图片的使用方法。

在以后的练习中,教师可以用各种各样的方式提醒学生如何进行练习,可是由于每项练习不同,尽管有些相似,教师还是不能假定即使没有说明,学生也总会知道如何去做。

2.1 分组

根据每项练习的要求和教师的需要,把学生分成几个小组,通常每组二至四人。教师为每个组提供练习的图片,每个组都用目的语进行练习。例如,"描述和比较"练习,一对学生彼此不能看对方手中的图片,只能用目的语口头比较两张相似但不完全相同的图片,目的就是找出这两张图片的每个不同之处。还有"看图说话"练习,每组学生用目的语共同讨论,根据几幅有连续情节的画面,一起讲述一个完整的故事。学生必须根据本组的图片一起商量,准备好本组的发言,然后向全班同学讲述。

在所有的练习中,教师都应该鼓励学生用他们自己的思想,尽可能创造性地完成练习的任务。

在所有的分组练习中,学生都只能使用目的语,尽管会有困难,例如词汇不足,但是学生要明确自己所要完成的练习任务,要学会用目的语交际。

对学生来说,分组练习是很有价值的。通过分小组,学生开始用他们学会的语言知识在他们现有水平上来完成练习任务。在这个令人愉快的传达真实信息的过程中,任务的完成会带给学生一种成就感。会使学生觉得所学到的是真实的、实用的东西,而且自己真正地能使用这些词语或结构来进行交际。

通过分小组练习,学生可以学习到语言的全部,而不仅仅只是词汇和句子结构。例如,他们学习如何变换角色,如何插话,如何停止,如何打断别人,如何讨论,以及如何在不知道准确词汇时描述和解释陌生的事物。这种带有语境的语言会帮助学生在交际时变得熟练自如。

分组练习提示

分组练习为学生的学习提供了很大益处。为了提高练习效率,下面有一些分组方法供教师参考:

(1)随意组合:让学生根据自己的语言能力或人际关系找到合适的同伴,这样学生可以选择身边的同学或朋友。有时这可以带来非常有效的结合,因为经常跟同样的人组合可以马上进入练习中,可以减少互相适应和调整时间;但不能每次只与固定的同伴练习,因为这样做会影响到练习的新鲜感和挑战性。

(2)教师指定:教师可以指定,告诉谁和谁一起练习。这样教师可以控制哪些人要在一起练习,有助于避免那些教师已知原因的有问题的组合。然而这样做有时会在师生之间产生不满或误会,比如,有时学生不喜欢变换所习惯的同伴,或不愿意跟老师指定的同伴练习等等。

(3) 寻找同伴:教师可以使用一种让学生按要求寻找同伴的方法。例如,可以让学生数数,然后号码相同的分为一组;还可以在发给学生前教师先把一个词或号码写在图片上,然后让学生找到和自己有同一个词或号码的同伴。这种不固定的组合有这样的优势,可以使学生每次都有新同伴,使他们面对带有新的交际模式的对象。因为必须用目的语来找到练习同伴,在这个过程中也有更多的交际练习。当然,这样做有时也有不足,比如分组要花较多时间,有时还会产生效率低的组合。

不管怎么分组,偶尔变换组合是很必要的。这样可以避免学生在每次练习时,只是简单地跟同一个人练习。

2.2 发言

虽然发言不像分组讨论那么重要,但是仍然为学生提供了一个明确练习任务和互相学习的好机会,而且还对练习起到检查和监督的作用。同时也给予学生一个展示自我水平的机会。(但是有的练习,像"描述和比较"就不需要一个发言步骤。)

教师应该要求学生的发言简明扼要。每项练习都有自己的发言方式,但是一般是一人或全组一起向全班讲述本组在讨论中一致同意的看法。发言者最好站在教室前边。像"看图说话"练习,每个组的一个人或几个人要根据教师发给的图片站在教室前边讲述一个短的故事。在讲述的过程中,讲述者可以举着图片,向全班同学指出有关的细节等等。最后,要给听的学生一些时间,使他们可以向发言者提问,澄清自己的疑问,或者就发言与图片矛盾的方面以及不合逻辑等方面提出异议。

教师应该这样鼓励学生,在别人发言时其他的学生应该注意听,要像观众一样参与进来。在每个组发言后,作为一种改善课堂气氛的方式,教师可以要求掌声鼓励,也可以提醒未发言的组注意听。

决定发言顺序有两个方法供教师参考:

(1) 学生自愿:由于是自愿,较好的学生会经常发言,为稍差的学生提供一个好的例子和榜样。然而这样也有一个不足,就是有些组总是首先发言,而有些稍差的组不注意听其他组的发言,只是用这个时间练习或准备自己的发言。

(2) 教师选择:教师选择小组发言,可以根据需要,特别掌握。教师可以为作榜样选择最好的组,也可以为鼓励选择最差的组;而且教师还可以选择那些总是不注意听别人发言的组,或在别人发言时继续练习的组。这样可以为发言者创造一种更好的、更受鼓舞的课堂气氛。

当一个组发言时,最好同组的每个人都说一部分,要求每个人准备,虽然这样通常要花较多时间,但是可以使每个人投入到练习中来。另一个意见是同组的每个成员都能根据教师的要求而准确地讲述,可以有一个代表很流利地讲述。这样做虽然较快,但是有时会使同组其他的人不好好准备(除了教师事先不告诉自己将要选择的人)。

2.3 总结练习

对于所有的练习,最后的总结活动都是重要而有用的。这通常是由教师控制的一个小的练习。教师从刚刚完成的练习中选择几个细节让全班讨论,或者与这些细节有关的内容,让学生口头练习;教师应适时把握练习控制权,给学生一种练习完成和结束的感觉。最后根据学生发言时出现的几个最主要的问题,教师应该给学生示范更恰当的结构和表达方式,或者介绍几个特别有用的词。

2.4 教师在练习中的角色

当学生分组练习时,教师应成为练习中一个既重要又活跃的角色。教师应该在各组间巡回监听学生的练习进展情况,同时向学生提供帮助或指导。通过在各组间巡回,依据对各组的简短的监听,教师可以得到学生对图片掌握情况的宝贵的信息反馈。那些不愿在全班同学面前问问题的学生会更愿意私下提出问题和寻求帮助。另外,教师还可以随时再次指导那些未按要求做练习或者有别的困难的学生。有时只用几句话,教师就可以帮助学生回到正确的练习途径中。

教师常发现的一些问题及改正方法:

(1)同一组的学生只有一个学生在起支配作用,在说话者和听话者之间缺少角色转换。

因为是交际练习,所以学生发出和输入信息都是很重要的,所有的学生都应该变换角色,参与讨论。教师可以用如下的方法帮助学生:教师可以问小组中那个不说话的学生练习进展得怎么样了,或者问他是否同意同伴所说的话等,通常这足以使那样的学生开始说话;另一种方法就是直接提醒那个组所要求的是自然变换交际角色。

(2)用母语而不用目的语。

通常有学生不明白这个练习最有价值的部分是分组讨论。有时他们只把最后的发言作为唯一的任务,而为了更快地达到这个目标就用母语来进行练习。为了克服上述这个弊端,教师必须保证学生在练习时只能使用目的语。教师可以直接提醒学生,而且要事先解释这个练习的目的所在,指出讨论对语言学习的重要性。这样才能使学生自觉地使用目的语进行分组讨论。

(3)练习缺乏进展。

一个组可能遇到障碍或失去练习的中心,教师可以用引导性的问题或明确的指示帮助他们继续进行。

(4)练习的方法不正确。

学生不可能总是准确理解练习的要求,特别是在第一次做每项练习的时候。此时教师的重新说明是很重要的,能很容易帮助学生改正练习方法。

2.5 练习的目的和应该使用的语言

这些练习的目的不是让学生说出完美的目的语来,而是使他们能用已经掌握的目的语以一种有意义的方式来交际。例如,在某些学习阶段的某些错误,只要能成功交际,就可以被接受(见3.交际法的基本原理)。学生不必像操母语的人那样准确地知道每个词或恰当的表达方式。教师可以鼓励学生使用间接策略来完成交际。教师不必事先提供每一个可能遇到的词,因为我们也希望学生学会在他们不知道一个规定的词汇时如何来完成交际。对学生来说,这是一种有效而实用的交际技巧。当学生问的时候,教师不是给出每个词,而是要帮助他们自己想出来,或者找到一种既不用这个词又能使之意思清楚的间接策略。当然很少的解答和难词可以事先写在黑板上,或者在练习中等学生问到时再写。学生很快就会习惯这种方法,当他们被难住时,就会很自然地看黑板寻找帮助。

3. 交际法的基本原理

3.1 导言和原理

交际法认为语言具有在个体间交互作用和交际的主要功能。不管哪种语言形式,无论是口语还是书面语,语言的社会功能都是让人们交互作用和交际。事实上,在一个社会里人们之间的所有交互作用都包括或以交际为基础。没有交际,社会就不会存在。用语言交际是人类所独有的一种特征,即交际是稳固建立在语言之上的。除了语言之外的交际形式(手势,面部表情,体态等等),交际的核心仍是以话语形式——语言出现。

(1)交际法的宗旨是(据 Richards & Rodgers, 1986, p. 71):
　　1)语言是意义的表层系统。
　　2)语言的主要功能是交互作用和交际。
　　3)语言的结构反映它的功能和交际作用。
　　4)语言的基本单位不仅仅是它的语法和结构特征,还应包括话语所体现的不同的功能和交际意义。
(2)语言的交互作用和交际功能是由七个基本的语言次功能构成,这是由幼年习得母语者得到的(Halliday, 1970, pp. 11 – 17):
　　1)工具功能:使用语言得到东西。
　　2)调控功能:使用语言控制别人的行为。
　　3)交互功能:使用语言与其他人发生交互作用。
　　4)个人功能:使用语言表达个人的感情和意思。
　　5)探索功能:使用语言来学习和发现。
　　6)想像功能:使用语言创造想像的世界。
　　7)表述功能:使用语言转换信息。
(3)依据这些宗旨,交际法作为一种教学思想,目标是(Richards & Rodgers, 1986, p. 66):
　　1)使交际能力成为语言教学的最终目标。
　　2)根据语言和交际不可分的原则来发展一些有助于四种语言技能(听、说、读、写)教学的技巧和方法。
(4)交际法认为交际是学习的一部分,而且学习语言的目的就是学会用这种语言交际。因此,语言教学的中心是交际能力,而不是仅仅掌握语言结构。交际能力包括四个方面(Richards & Rodgers, 1986, p.71):
　　1)语法能力:语法和词汇能力。
　　2)社会语言能力:了解交际场景的能力。(包括角色关系,各个角色共有的信息,以及交际的目的。)
　　3)对话能力:了解对话中各种要素之间相互关系的能力以及根据对话的需要,如何传播信息的能力。
　　4)策略能力:在交际时,如何开始,如何结束,如何继续,如何补充修改,如何转变话题的能力。

值得注意的是,语法能力事实上是很多传统语言教学法唯一的核心。的确,在第二语言学习中,普遍存在着一个问题,就是学了很多年第二语言的学生,仍然不能用这种语言与人交际。就是为了解决这个问题,所以创造了语言教学中的交际法。交际法试着把语言融入在更为广阔的真实的社会文化的语境之中。理想的使用交际法的课堂是学生在学习如何使用目的语与人进行高效的、真正的、成功的交际。

3.2 交际法的实际应用

交际法最基本的宗旨是学习者必须是通过使用语言来学习语言。虽然准确的词汇、结构和功能等等的教学有用而且必要,但是使学习者去使用那些被教的有益于学习的内容是更有益的,只是简单地记忆生词和句子形式等是远远不够的。设计交际活动和练习要尽可能地遵循下列原则:
　　(1)交际原则:任何包括真实交际的活动都有助于语言学习。
　　(2)任务原则:用语言来进行有实际意义的活动都有助于语言学习。

(3)实际意义原则:对学习者有实际意义的学习内容有助于学习。

虽然交际活动有很多种,但是这些活动通常都应该含有信息差异。在交际中,一个信息一方有,而另一方没有,此时信息差异就产生了。在这个具有信息差异的练习过程中,必须使用目的语来传递信息,完成消除信息差异的任务。由此可见,信息差异的练习非常符合上面所列的原则(1)和原则(2)。由于信息被传递,要与别人交际,真正的交际就会产生,这就符合原则(1)的交际要求。消除信息差异是一种具体的、有限制的并且有意义的任务,这就符合原则(2)的任务要求。值得注意的就是在同样的练习中,如果交际双方都拥有相同的信息(也就是说没有信息差异),那么这些练习就会违背原则(1)和原则(2),就会失去练习意义。

交际法有很多长处,特别是信息差异的练习,在交际成功时,学生可以获得成就感。当他们传递信息、消除信息差异时,他们发现语言确实在工作,语言不只是一系列的无生命的符号或代码(口头的或书面的)。他们发现对他们来说一种陌生而比较难学的外语是有用的,并且这种语言确实履行了重要的社会功能。

在交际法中,交际很早就开始;交际出现在任何水平,甚至在学习初期,学生只学了最基本的词汇后。简单的交际应受到鼓励,老师希望学生在他们现有的水平上使用语言。虽然一个学生只学了很有限的词汇、语法和一点交际技巧,这个学生也应受到鼓励,让他尽可能地表达出来。如果这个学生的水平更高,那么他能用更高的水平交际。交际法不认为一个学习者在开始使用这种语言之前必须先学习掌握它。

3.3 交际策略

第二语言学习者通常会使用一些交际策略,这些策略可以分为两大类,直接策略和间接策略。如下所示:

(1)直接策略:

当学习者对要讲的内容有足够的语言能力时,就会用恰当的话语来直接表达出来。

(2)间接策略:

当学习者不知道如何用恰当的话语来直接表达时,就会采取以下间接的表达形式来帮助达到交际目标:

1)近似替代:

当学习者不知道如何准确地表达出来某个意思时,就会用一个明知不准确,但意思相近的词或语言结构等来替代,以此来满足表达的需要。(如用"面包"代替"馒头","选择"代替"选举"。)

2)创造词汇:

为了表达某个概念,学习者会创造一个新的词。(如用"语言历史"代表"语言学","飞机公司"代表"航空公司"。)

3)解释说明:

学习者会描述说明事物的功能或形式来完成交际任务。(如用"可以去月球上的飞机"代表"航天飞机","有三个轮子的自行车"代表"三轮车"。)

4)逐字翻译:

将母语意思直接翻译成目的语。(如"他放菜在我的盘子上"="他给我夹菜"。)

5)换用母语:

在表达中用母语词汇来替代目的语词汇。(如"我去发一个fax〈传真〉"。)

6)寻求帮助:

在表达中寻求对方的帮助。(如"这个汉语怎么说?")

7)手势表演：

用非语言形式来表达意思。(如用拍手的动作来表示"鼓掌"。)

8)逃避话题：

当学习者对要讲的内容没有足够的语言能力时,就会避免谈论此话题。(如上课提问时,不主动回答问题,或课外避免出现在讲某些话题的场合,或在交际中转换话题。)

9)终止表达：

当学习者在表达中发现对要讲的内容没有足够的语言能力时,就会终止表达。

第一类,直接策略是被理想化的、"完美"的交际。确实我们很希望我们的学生能成功地直接表达,因此教师习惯上把所看到的间接表达当做学生缺乏交际能力的表现。然而,果真如此吗？请注意,即使对一个操母语者而言,也不能用直接表达来描述下面的四个图形,他们也不得不使用间接策略3)来解释说明。

□　○　＊　A

事实上,如果我们在操母语者之中寻找真正的交际,我们会发现大部分间接策略偶尔或习惯性地被使用。当然其中明显有三个策略不会被操母语者使用,而且都被确认为是病态的策略,这就是：5)换用母语；8)逃避话题；9)终止表达。这些策略当然应该被禁止,但是我们应该允许学生使用其余的策略,甚至教他们学习使用这些策略,因为这是成功交际必不可少的一部分。

3.4 准确性和偏误

儿童学习第一语言和成人学习第二语言的方式有很大的不同。一个特别显著的差别就是熟练程度水平即学习者最后获得的综合能力。我们知道除了病态情况以外,事实上所有的儿童都能学会他们自己的语言。当然,即使是母语学习者,他们达到的流利水平、掌握的词汇等也会因人而异,但是差别幅度不大。

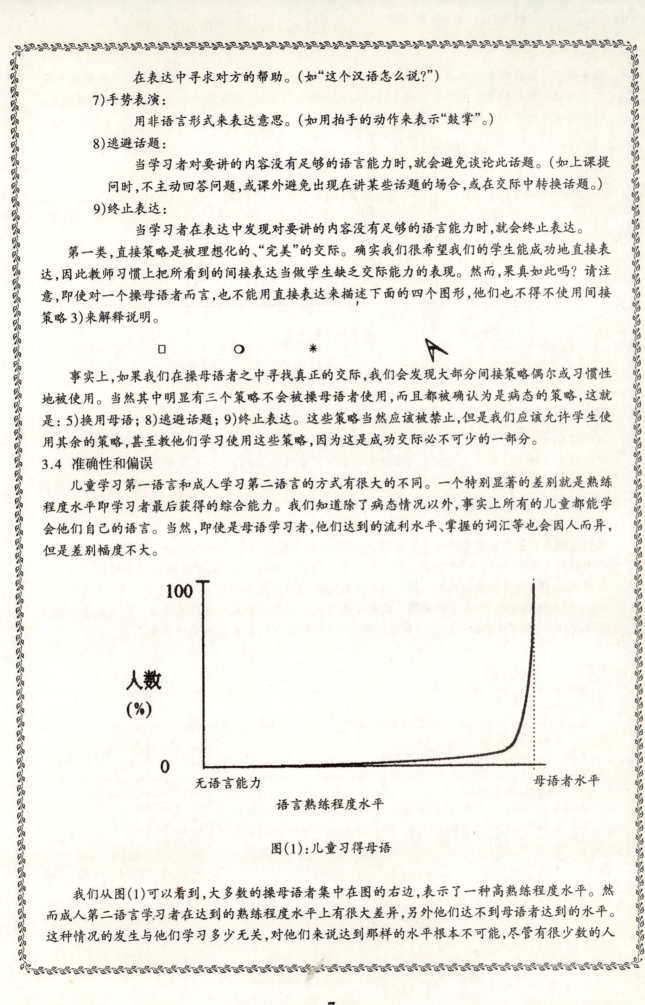

图(1)：儿童习得母语

我们从图(1)可以看到,大多数的操母语者集中在图的右边,表示了一种高熟练程度水平。然而成人第二语言学习者在达到的熟练程度水平上有很大差异,另外他们达不到母语者达到的水平。这种情况的发生与他们学习多少无关,对他们来说达到那样的水平根本不可能,尽管有很少数的人确实接近它。大部分第二语言学习者能在适宜的条件下做得相当好,达到相当好的熟练程度水平,但是也有极少数的学生不管付出多大的努力或条件如何优越,都不能掌握目的语。图(2)显示更多的学习者集中于钟型曲线的中部。

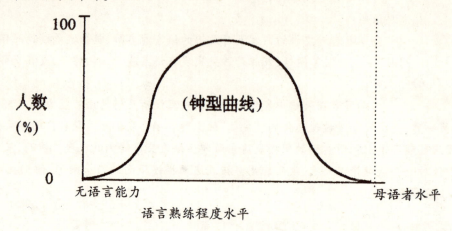

图(2):成人学习第二语言

由于我们知道成年学习者根本不能达到母语者的能力水平,那么我们为什么还把"完美"作为教学目标?交际法所持有的观点就是应该教学习者用目的语有效交际,即使一些学习者从来没用目的语真正解决过困难。虽然我们希望和鼓励使用准确的目的语,但是我们最重要的目的是让学生获得有效的交际能力。因此在交际法中,我们的目标从来不是完美的准确性,因为这是不能达到的,所以才只是要求学习者达到一种较高的准确度,然而更要求学生拥有相当高的交际能力。

虽然限于篇幅,在此不能详细讨论,但是事实上偏误是可以接受的,它们是学习过程中不可避免的。因为在第二语言习得研究中证明,学习者在语言学习过程中存在着一种介于母语与目的语之间的独立语言系统,叫"中介语",然而它又是一种动态的语言系统,是随着学习者的语言学习及交际需要不断向目的语靠拢的。因此教师不需总是担心避免每个学习者的每个偏误,在实际过程中,一种个体的学习中,真正的偏误一定会出现。教师改正也会发现这样的事实——不是每次偏误都需要改正,教师要根据学生学习周期特殊阶段,从能改正的最重要的偏误着手。

参考书:

Halliday, M. A. K. (1975). *Learning How to Mean: Explorations in the Development of Language*. London: Edward Arnold.

Larsen-Freeman, Diane and Michael H. Long (1991). *An Introduction to Second Language Acquisition Research*. New York: Longman Inc.

Palmer, Adrian S., et al (1985). *Back & Forth: Pair Activities for Language Development*. New Jersey: Alemany Press.

Richards, Jack C. and Theodore S. Rodgers (1986). *Approaches and Methods in Language Teaching*. Cambridge: Cambridge University Press.

Winn-Bell Olsen, Judy (1984). *Look Again Pictures*. New Jersey: Alemany Press.

Yorkey, Richard (1985). *Talk-A-Tivities*. Massachussetts: Adison-Wesley Publishing Company.

Learning to Speak
Picture-based Communicative Activities for the Language Classroom

Preface

1. Introduction

This book contains a series of six types of picture-based exercises for classroom use. Based on principles of Communicative Language Teaching (CLT; see Section 3), these exercises are designed to help students learn to communicate in the target language effectively. Through various formats, the exercises compel students to speak and communicate in the target language with their classmates in small groups. The exercises, with clearly defined tasks and completion points, are interesting and motivating, allow a great level of student determination, and lead to rich and varied classroom experiences.

Throughout all, the student uses the target language as a tool to finish communicative tasks. It is during this motivated process of carrying out tasks that practice and learning occurs.

The exercises are suitable for all class types and can be used with any language teaching methodologies that encourage speaking and communicative practice. The exercises are also suitable for all language levels — the student uses whatever amount of language already mastered to accomplish the task of the exercise at his or her own level. In addition to the broader communicative elements inherent in the exercises (see Section 3 for more on these elements), they also contain a broad range of vocabulary and grammatical forms — from household contexts to hospitals, from parks to buses — and different situations and actions — leading to progressive, existential, locative, directional, and many other forms and constructs. In addition to practising communicative macro skills, students also practise important finer skills — speaking, listening, and reading.

The exercises are multi-faceted, with both teacher-directed whole-class portions (relatively short), and completely student-driven small group portions (longer).

Since these are *information gap* exercises, the book should not be issued directly to the student. Instead, the teacher should tear out and issue each one at the time it is to be used. Since this is also intended to be a source-book for teachers and other educators, the exercises can also be photocopied for use by the *purchasing* individual teacher.

This book contains six types of exercises (described in more detail in each section):

1) *Ordering Pictures I & II* (26 exercises total, 52 pages)

    Without looking at their partner's sheet, student pairs match up the order of small pictures on two separate sheets.

2) *Comparing Pictures* (10 exercises, 20 pages)

    Without looking at their partner's picture, student pairs compare similar but not identical pictures in order to discover differences.

3) *Drawing a Picture* (12 exercises, 6 pages)

    In pairs, one student holds a picture that the other cannot see, and describes it while the other student draws it based on the oral description.

4) *Telling a Story* (20 exercises, 20 pages)

In small groups students discuss a series of pictures and come up with a single description or story based on the events shown in the pictures.

5) *Creating a Story* (10 exercises, 10 pages)

In small groups students discuss a series of pictures and create a single story based on the pictures.

6) *Discussing a Topic I & II* (12 exercises total, 9 pages)

In small groups students discuss interesting topics provided in picture form.

Within each type and where possible, the exercises are roughly ordered from easiest to hardest. In addition, each type has its own detailed instructions (each with *Purpose*, *Procedure*, and *Important Points* sections), and a special *Example Page* that the teacher can use the first time through to help in the all important explanation of the exercise to students.

2. Teacher Explanation and Introduction to the Exercises

It is, of course, vital that the instructor gives a good explanation of the exercise to the students before carrying it out. This is especially important the first time through, but is also important subsequent times. Much classroom time and student frustration can be saved by a careful explanation, and without it everything is less successful.

The first time through, the instructor should use the sample page, provided with each exercise, to walk through the exercise with the class. Each set of instructions contains suggestions about how this might be done.

Subsequently, the instructor can use various methods to remind the students how to do the exercise. However, since each type of material is different, yet somewhat similar, the instructor should not assume that the students will always know what to do without explanation.

2.1 Group Work

In group work the students are split into a certain number of groups, usually having 2 to 4 students each, depending on the requirements of the specific exercise and the needs of the teacher. Each group gets together and gets materials provided by the teacher. Together the group carries out the activity using the target language. For example, in *Comparing Pictures*, a pair of people compare two similar but not identical pictures verbally, using only the target language, while not looking at the picture held by their partner, with the goal of finding each picture difference. For *Telling a Story*, a small group of three people discuss, in the target language, a series of pictures that together make up a story or event. Together they work out and agree upon their own single group interpretation of the pictures for later presentation to the whole class.

In all exercises the teacher should encourage the students to be creative and to use their own ideas — as long as they follow and fulfill the requirements of the exercise.

During all parts of group work the students are required to use the target language solely, and to figure out ways of accomplishing their goal, even when difficulties, such as lack of certain vocab, arise. Students must learn to communicate in the target language.

Group work is the most valuable part of the exercise for the students. Through group work students get to use the language that they have learned, at whatever level of proficiency, to acomplish something. Actual information is transferred between participants in a gratifying way, with accomplishment as the reward. This shows to the students that what they have been learning is real, that it has a function and purpose, and that they can actually use it themselves to accomplish something.

Through group work students learn the full range of language, not just words and sentence patterns. They learn how to take turns, how to start an interaction, or how to stop, or stop someone else, how to discuss, and how to describe or explain something unfamiliar (without exact vocabulary items sometimes). This contextualizes language, and helps students to become proficient at communicating.

Group Work Hints

Group work provides great benefits to student learning. There are several ways that the instructor can split the students intos groups with different benefits:

a) *Naturally*: Have the students find the appropriate number of partners based on their own abilities. This often means that they will pick someone closeby, or a friend, and will be unlikely to switch partners throughout the term of study. Sometimes this leads to very effective and efficient matchings, and decreases time needed for partners to adjust to each other.

b) *Teacher assign*: The teacher can set up the groups, telling which student to work together. This allows the teacher to quickly get things started, and to control who work together. This helps to avoid matchings that the teacher already knows are problematic for whatever reasons. However, students may not always like the teacher-assigned groupings.

c) *Randomly*: The teacher can use a method that matches students randomly. This can be done, for example, by having the students count off by numbers then finding people with the same number, or it could be done by the teacher first putting a word or number on the materials before handing them out. Then the students would find the person(s) with the same word. Random assignment has the advantage of putting the students with new people each time, and thus exposing them to new language patterns, etc. It also allows more communicative practice since the process of finding partners is also done in the target language. It has the disadvantage that it is slower, and sometimes creates inefficient student matchings.

Regardless of how groups are made, it is important to occasionally change the groups so that students do not simply work with the same person throughout the term.

2.2 Presentations

Although presentations are not as important as group discussion, they still provide a good opportunity for students to practise and learn from each other. They also provide a set of clear tasks, and motivation as students usually want to show what they can do.

The teacher should require the presentations to be short and to the point. Each type of activity has its own type of presentation, but they usually follow the pattern of having one or more members of the group tell the whole class (preferably while standing in front of the class) what the group agree upon during discussion of the materials. So, in the case of '*Telling a Story*' one or more members would tell a short story in front of the class based on the materials that the group had received from the teacher. During the telling of the story, whoever is speaking can hold the materials and point out to the class relevant details, etc. At the end, the students who have been listening should be given time to ask for clarification from the speaker(s), or to challenge the speaker on areas that seem to contradict the materials, or do not seem logical, or well organized, etc.

During presentations the other students should listen and take part as an audience, and the teacher should encourage this. The teacher may want to encourage applause after each presentation as a way of improving classroom atmosphere. The teacher should remind non-presenting groups to pay attention to the speakers.

There are two usual ways to decide which group starts the first presentation:

a) *Ask for volunteers*: By asking for volunteers the better students will often go first, and thus provide a good example and model for the weaker students. However, it is not advantageous that the same groups always go first, and some weaker groups may not listen to the presentation, instead using the time to continue practising or working out their own presentations.

b) *Teacher pick*: When the teacher picks the group he or she can control specifically based on needs. He or she can pick the best groups (to allow modelling), or the weakest groups (as encouragement), or the teacher can pick groups that habitually do not listen well (or tend to continue to practise during other people's presentations), thus creating a better and more supportive classroom atmosphere for other presenters.

When groups give presentations, it is usually best to have all members speak for part of the presentation, requiring everyone to prepare, although this usually takes more time. Another option is to have one person speak for the whole group, providing a fairly smooth speech. But sometimes this means that other members do not prepare as well (unless the teacher does not tell which one he or she will select to speak ahead of time).

2.3 Ending Activity

With all of these exercises it is important and useful to do a final summary activity. This is usually a teacher-driven short activity, where the teacher picks a few aspects of the just-finished exercise and has the class discuss, or otherwise perform some oral activity related to those aspects as a large group. This gives control back to the teacher, and provides students with a feeling of accomplishment and closure. It is also a great chance for the teacher to gently model a few correct forms where mistakes were previously observed, or introduce a few especially useful vocabulary words.

2.4 Teacher's Role During Activities

While students are working in groups carrying out these activities, the teacher has a very important and active role. The teacher should move among the groups and monitor their progress, and provide them with help or hints as needed. The teacher, by moving around through the groups, can get precious feedback about how well the students have mastered certain material by simply quietly listening for a short time at each group. At the same time, students who often do not feel comfortable asking questions in front of the whole class will be more likely to privately ask questions and seek help. Additionally, the teacher can redirect students who are not doing the exercise correctly, or are having other difficulties. Just a few words by the teacher can, at times, help the students to get back on track.

Some common problems for the teacher to look for, and correct:

a) *One student dominating the group, or lack of role switching between speaker and listener within a group*:

Since this is a communicative activity it is important that students partake in the full give-and-take of communication, and all speakers should take turns in discussion. The teacher can help here in several ways. The teacher could ask a non-speaking member of the group how progress is going, or if they agree with the person speaking, etc. Oftentimes this is enough to start the other members speaking. Another option is to just remind the group that natural turn-taking is expected.

b) *Use of language other than target language*:

Often students do not understand that the group work/discussion portion of the exercise is the most valuable, and is where the best practice and learning occurs. Sometimes they see the endresult(usually presentation) as the only goal, and thus attempt to short-cut via better-learned languages. The teacher must work to ensure that students only use the target language throughout the process. The teacher can remind the students of the requirement for target language only, and explain, beforehand, what the exercise is really about, with the importance of the discussion.

c) *Lack of progress*:

A group may get stalled, or may lose focus of the goal of the exercise. The teacher can help them get going again with leading questions or explicit instructions.

d) *Not doing the right thing*:

Students may not always understand exactly what is expected, especially the first time with a type of exercise. Again, the teacher is very important here, and can easily help the students to get back on track.

What Kind of Language Should They Use?

The goal of these exercises is not that students speak the target language perfectly, but rather that they use whatever amount of target language that they have already learned to interact in a meaningful manner. Thus, certain types of mistakes, during certain learning stages, are acceptable as long as they can successfully communicate (see CLT section). Students do not need to know every word or express things exactly as a native speaker — they can and should be encouraged to improvise. There is no need for the teacher to provide an exhaustive vocabulary list, and indeed that is counterproductive since we want students to learn to communicate even when they do not know a specific word. This is an important and useful skill for students. The teacher should not give every word when asked, but instead help the students to remember the words themselves, or to find a way of expressing the concept without the word (circumlocution), although, some tie in to previously or just taught vocab is always good, of course. A few key and difficult vocabulary words can be written on the board ahead of time, or during the exercise as students bring them to the teacher's attention — students will soon get used to this method, and naturally look to the board when they are stuck.

3. Brief Overview of Communicative Language Teaching (CLT)

3.1 Introduction and Principles

Communicative Language Teaching (CLT) springs from the belief that the primary function of language is interaction and communication between individuals. Regardless of form, whether spoken or written, language is used for the social function of allowing people to interact and communicate. Indeed, virtually all interactions between people in a society are based on, or contain, communication. No society could even exist without communication. The ability to communicate effectively defines the human race. Communication, in turn, is based firmly in language. Despite forms of extra-linguistic communication (hand gestures, facial expressions, body posture, etc.), the core of communication is still manifested in linguistic form: language. This is thus a belief that (inspired by Richards & Rogers, 1986, p.71):

1) Language is a system for the expression of meaning.

2) The primary function of language is for interaction and communication.

3) The structure of language reflects its functional and communicative uses.

4) The primary units of language are not merely its grammatical and structural features, but categories of

functional and communicative meaning as exemplified in discourse.

The interactional and communicative function of language is made up of seven basic subfunctions of language that are learned by native speakers even at the earliest years of childhood (Halliday, 1970, pp. 11-17):

1) *the instrumental function*: using language to get things;
2) *the regulatory function*: using language to control the behavior of others;
3) *the interactional function*: using language to create interaction with others;
4) *the personal function*: using language to express personal feelings and meanings;
5) *the heuristic function*: using language to learn and discover;
6) *the imaginative function*: using language to create a world of the imagination;
7) *the representational function*: using language to transfer information.

Then, with these beliefs in mind, Communicative Language Teaching was created as an approach that aims to (Richards & Rodgers, 1986, p.66):

1) make communicative competence the goal of language teaching; and
2) develop procedures for teaching four language skills that acknowledge the interdependence of language and communication.

Thus, communication is both part of learning and goal — learning a language is learning to communicate in this approach. The focus of language teaching is on communicative competence, rather than on mere mastery of structures. Communicative competence itself has four dimensions (Richards & Rodgers, 1986, p.71):

1) *grammatical competence*: grammatical and lexical capability.
2) *sociolinguistic competence*: understanding of social context in which communication takes place, including role relationships, the shared information of the participants, and the communicative purpose for their interaction;
3) *discourse competence*: interpretation of elements in terms of interconnectedness and how meaning is represented in relationship to the entire discourse or text;
4) *strategic competence*: coping strategies that communicators employ to initiate, terminate, maintain, repair, and redirect communication.

Notice that item 1), grammatical competence, is virtually the sole focus of many (traditional) types of language teaching. Indeed, CLT is, in part, a response to the too often seen problem of students who have studied a second language (in terms of grammatical competence) for many years yet can still not communicate with other people in that language. CLT tries to take language in within its broader realworld sociocultural context. Ideally, the CLT classroom is an environment where students learn how to carry out efficient, effective, and successful communication with other people in the target language.

3.2 Some Practical Aspects of CLT

A fundamental belief in CLT is that a learner must use a language in order to learn it. Although explicit teaching of vocabulary, structure, and function, etc. is useful and necessary, it is also vital to have learners use the items that they are instructed about in ways that are conducive to learning. It is simply not enough to just memorize words or sentence types, etc. Thus CLT activities and exercises are designed as much as possible with the following over-arching principles in mind:

1) *Communication principle*: Activities that involve real communication promote learning.
2) *Task principle*: Activities in which language is used for carrying out meaningful tasks promote learn-

ing.

3) *Meaningfulness principle*: Learning content that is meaningful to the learner supports the learning process.

Although CLT activities take many forms, activities frequently contain an *information gap*. An information gap exists when one person has information that another person does not have. During an information gap exercise, language (the target language) must be used to pass information, and thus finish the task of eliminating the information gap. Notice how well information gap exercises conform to principles 1) and 2) above: Real communication must occur [principle 1)] since information must be transferred or communicated to another person, and the elimination of the information gap is a specific, quantifiable and meaningful task [principle 2)]. Note that the same exercises, but where all parties share the same information (that is, without the information gap), no longer conform to principles 1) and 2), and are thus much less meaningful.

One advantage of CLT, and information gap exercises in particular, is the feeling of accomplishment that the students get when communication is successful — as they transfer information and close the information gap they discover that language actually works, that language is not just a series of lifeless signs or codes (spoken or written). They discover that a foreign language — strange and inaccessible to them — is useful and does indeed perform important social functions.

In CLT communication starts early, and occurs at whatever level possible. Even at very early stages, after even the most basic vocabulary is learned, simple communication is encouraged. Students are expected to use language at whatever level they are at. If a student has only learned a limited vocabulary, grammar, and a few communicative skills, the student is still encouraged to express him or herself as well as possible; if the student's level is higher then the student can communicate at that higher level. In CLT there is no belief that a learner must first master the language being learned in order to start using it.

3.3 Communicative Strategies

Learners employ a number of communicative strategies. These strategies can be split into two major categories, *direct* and *indirect strategies*. These are listed below (based on Larsen-Freeman & Long, 1991, p.127).

I. *Direct strategies*

When the learner has sufficient capability in the target language to express the desired content, he or she uses appropriate language to express meaning directly.

II. *Indirect strategies*

1) Approximation

When the learner does not know exactly how to express a meaning correctly, the learner uses a single target-language vocabulary item or structure which the learner knows is not correct, but which shares enough semantic features in common with the desired item to satisfy the speaker (e.g., 'pipe' for 'waterpipe').

2) Word coinage

The learner makes up a new word in order to communicate a desired concept (e.g., 'airball' for 'balloon').

3) Circumlocution

The learner describes the characteristics or elements of the object or action instead of using the appropriate target language structure (e.g., 'a bicycle with three wheels' for 'tricycle').

4) Literal translation

The learner translates word for word from the native language (e.g., 'He invites him to drink' for 'They toast one another').

5) Language switch

The learner uses the native language term without bothering to translate (e.g., 'balon' for 'balloon', or 'tirtil' for 'caterpillar').

6) Appeal for assistance

The learner asks for the correct term or structure (e.g., 'What is this?').

7) Mime

The learner uses non-verbal strategies in place of meaning structure (e.g., clapping one's hands to illustrate applause).

8) Topic avoidance

The learner simply does not talk about concepts for which the vocabulary or other meaning structure is not known (e.g., not actively answering questions in class, or, outside of class, avoiding circumstances that might require discussion of certain topics, or suddenly changing topics mid-utterance).

9) Message abandonment

During communication, the learner discovers a lack of meaning structure related to certain content, has difficulty, and stops mid-utterance.

The first strategy, direct communication, is the idealized 'perfect' communication. And, indeed, we do hope that our students can successfully communicate directly. But teachers have traditionally seen many of the indirect strategies as problems, that is, as showing weakness in student communication skills. But are they really? Notice that even for a native speaker, not all of the following four shapes can be described using direct communication. Indeed, even the native speaker has to resort to the indirect strategy of explaining [number 3) above]:

○   ❑   *   ⌁

In fact, if we look at actual communication among native speakers we find that most of these indirect strategies are employed either occasionally, or on a regular basis. Indeed, there are only three of the strategies above that are typically not used by native speakers, or all considered markedly dysfunctional, numbers 5), 8),9)('using L1 words,' 'avoid a topic,''stopping'). These strategies should be discouraged. However we should allow our students to use the remaining strategies, and even teach them. They are a vital part of successful communication.

3.4 Accuracy and Errors

There are great differences in the way children learn their first language, and the way that an adult learns a second language. One especially obvious difference is the level of proficiency, or over-all ability, ultimately attained by the learner. We know that virtually all children, except in pathological circumstances, learn to speak their own language as a child. There is some difference among even native learners as to the level of fluency attained, and vocabulary, etc., the range is, however, quite narrow. We can see this in Graph 1, where the huge majority of speakers cluster to the right of the graph, representing a high level of proficiency. However adult L2 learners vary greatly in the level of proficiency attained. Additionally, they fall short of the level attained by native speakers. This happens no matter how much they study. It is simply impossible for them to reach that level, although a very few do approach it. Most second language learners can do fairly well under the right circumstances, gaining a proficiency at a fairly good level, although a few students will never gain any mastery regardless of effort and environment. This is shown in Graph 2, where we see more learners clustering in the middle, in a traditional Bell-curve.

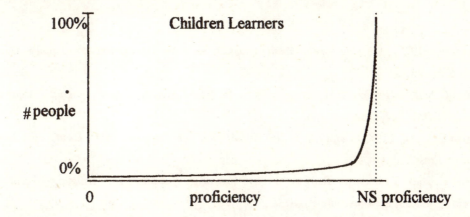

Graph 1: Child native-language learner proficiency

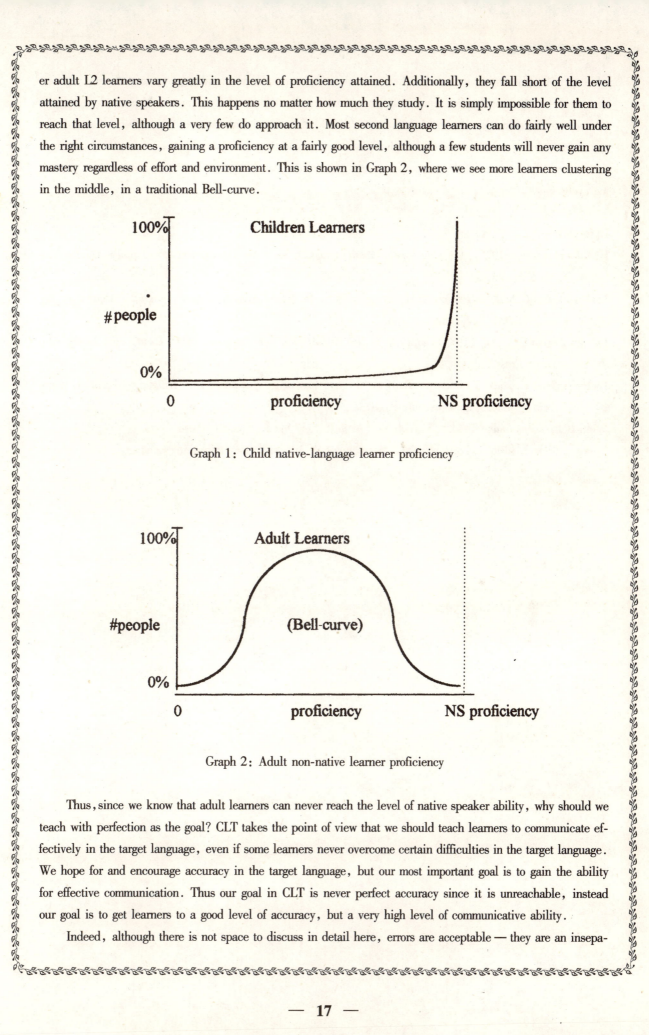

Graph 2: Adult non-native learner proficiency

Thus, since we know that adult learners can never reach the level of native speaker ability, why should we teach with perfection as the goal? CLT takes the point of view that we should teach learners to communicate effectively in the target language, even if some learners never overcome certain difficulties in the target language. We hope for and encourage accuracy in the target language, but our most important goal is to gain the ability for effective communication. Thus our goal in CLT is never perfect accuracy since it is unreachable, instead our goal is to get learners to a good level of accuracy, but a very high level of communicative ability.

Indeed, although there is not space to discuss in detail here, errors are acceptable — they are an inseparable part of the learning process. Teachers need not always worry about avoiding every learner error. At certain periods in an individual's learning, certain errors are expected, as a natural part of their interlanguage development. The correction of errors by the teacher should also reflect this reality — not every error needs to be corrected each time; instead the teacher should start with significant errors that are correctable (that is, where the learner is able to accept the teacher input and put it to use) at that particular stage in the student's learning cycle.

References:

Halliday, M. A. K. (1975). *Learning How to Mean: Explorations in the Development of Language*. London: Edward Arnold.

Larsen-Freeman, Diane and Michael H. Long (1991). *An Introduction to Second Language Acquisition Research*. New York: Longman Inc.

Palmer, Adrian S., et al (1985). *Back & Forth: Pair Activities for Language Development*. New Jersey: Alemany Press.

Richards, Jack C., and Theodore S. Rodgers (1986). *Approaches and Methods in Language Teaching*. Cambridge: Cambridge University Press.

Winn-Bell Olsen, Judy (1984). *Look Again Pictures*. New Jersey: Alemany Press.

Yorkey, Richard (1985). *Talk-A-Tivities*. Massachussetts: Adison-Wesley Publishing Company.

练　习

一、描述和排列(一)、(二)

练习目的

这项练习提供 A、B 两张有成行小图的图片,A、B 的每行小图画面完全相同,但顺序不同。要求学生根据所定的听、说顺序逐行轮流描述和排列。一人描述,另一人比较画面内容,来排列此行画面的顺序。这项练习除了训练学生的交际能力外,还着重于词汇和短句的练习。练习(一)有 8 行,每行 4 幅小图,更着重于词汇练习;练习(二)有 4 行,每行 5 幅小图,更着重于短句练习。

使用说明

将学生分成若干组,每组两人。他们分别拿着图片 A 和图片 B,互相不能看对方的图片。教师按照所定的听、说顺序让学生轮流描述和排列,听者在排列时可以将序号写在空白的圆圈内。如果一方的描述不够清楚明白,另一方不能进行排列时,要马上向对方提出问题,来帮助自己进行排列。

注意事项

首次做这项练习时,教师应先举例说明练习方法。手举为举例而准备的图片,给学生展示,上面分别印有图片 A 和图片 B。请学生进行描述,并且同时比较其与另一张图片画面顺序的差别。教师在举例说明时,要简短清楚,时间最好控制在 5 分钟之内。

学生进行分组练习时,因为语言水平有高有低,练习速度有快有慢,各组自然不会同时完成。教师要善于观察学生的练习情况。当大部分学生已经完成,只有个别组的学生还没结束时,教师就要选择时机,结束这次练习。如果要大部分学生来等的话,就会使这些学生产生浪费时间的感觉,影响学生的学习积极性。如果有个别学生很快完成练习时,教师可允许他们用目的语自由交谈。

练习进行完后,教师最好进行一个简短的总结。常用的方法分为两步:首先教师将本次练习所使用的图片 A 和图片 B 同时展示给学生,请学生一起描述和排列;然后,抓住图片中的一个关键内容,提出一个有趣的问题,请学生自由发表意见。这样既可以检查练习效果,给学生一个互相学习、发挥自己的机会,又可以增加练习趣味性,提高学生的学习积极性。

EXERCISES

1. **Ordering Pictures I & II**

Purpose:

In this exercise students in pairs are provided with two sheets, 'A' and 'B', each containing rows of small pictures. The pictures on pages A and B are identical, except that their order in each row is different. The students take turns for each row, as indicated on each sheet, describing and listening. As one person describes, the other compares his or her pictures, and orders the pictures to match the order being described. Besides for practising overall communicative ability, this exercise is also especially good for vocabulary and short phrase practice. Type I has eight rows per page, with four pictures per row, and emphasizes vocabulary practice; type II has four rows per page, with five pictures per row, and emphasizes short phrases.

Procedure:

Separate the students into groups, two people per group, one person with sheet A and the other with sheet B. Each person cannot look directly at the other person's sheet. In turns, the students describe and listen to determine the proper order of pictures in each row. The person listening numbers the pictures in the row to match the other being spoken in the small blank circle provided on each picture. If the listener cannot figure out the proper order then that person should immediately ask questions of the speaker for clarification.

Important Points:

The first time through this exercise the instructor should go through an example trial run, using the provided example sheet (marked for both A and B roles on a single sheet), to show how the exercise should be carried out. The teacher should hold the example sheet before the class, and ask students to describe, while at the same time comparing differences in order between A and B. The trial run should be simple and clear, and should be kept under five minutes.

Because of differences in target language level within a given group, some groups will progress quickly, and some slowly, and will finish the exercise at different times. The instructor should monitor the progress of the exercise closely, and end the exercise when most of the groups have finished, and just one or two groups have not quite finished. If most groups have to wait too long, they will feel that they are wasting time and this will affect the students' attitudes towards the exercise. If a few students finish very early, they can be allowed to chat in the target language.

After completion, the instructor should carry out a short summary exercise. Usually this contains two steps. First, the instructor can take sheets A and B and show them to the class and have them describe and order a few rows. Afterwards, the instructor can pick a significant item or two from the pictures and bring up some interesting questions, and have the students give their opinions. This allows the instructor to check up on the exercise results, gives students an opportunity to learn from each other, and allows them to express themselves. It also makes the exercise more interesting, and increases the degree of student activeness.

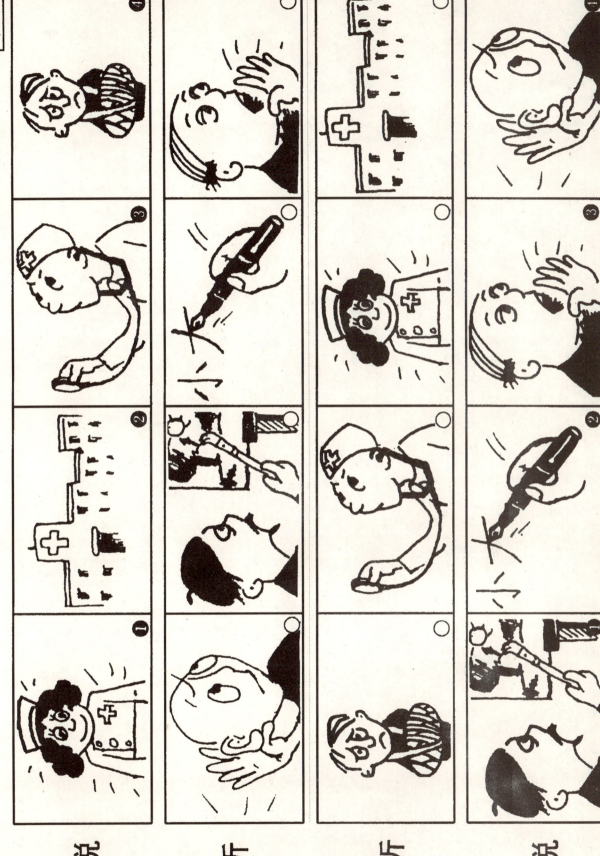

描述和排列 （一） 1A

1. 说	❶	❷	❸	❹
2. 听	八 ○	一 ○	六 ○	四 ○
3. 说	❶	❷	❸	❹
4. 听	○	○	○	○
5. 说	❶	❷	❸	❹
6. 听	○	○	○	○
7. 说	❶	❷	❸	❹
8. 听	○	○	○	○

描述和排列 （一） 1B

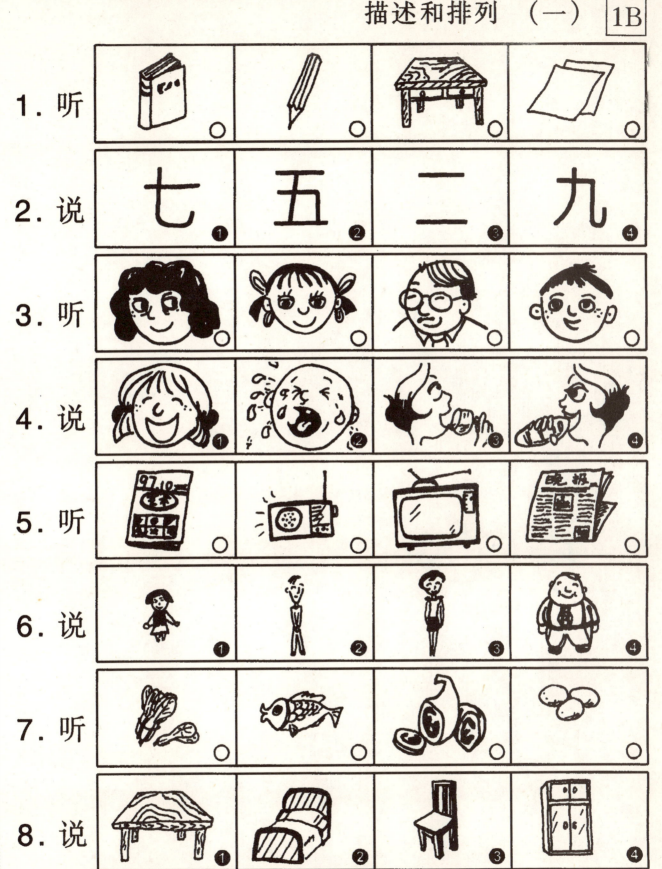

描述和排列 （一） 2A

1. 说　九① 三② 零③ 十④

2. 听

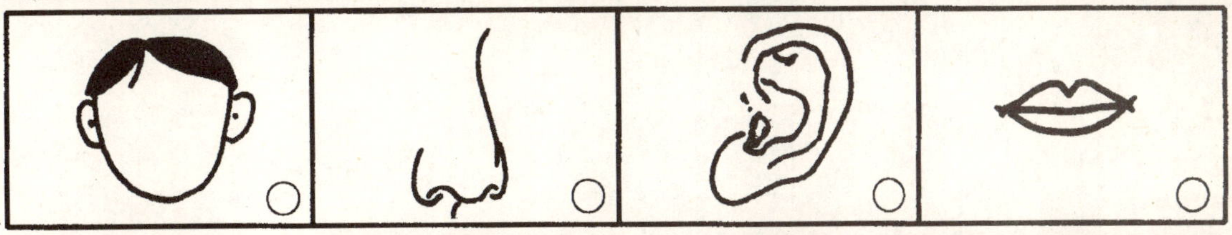

3. 说

4. 听

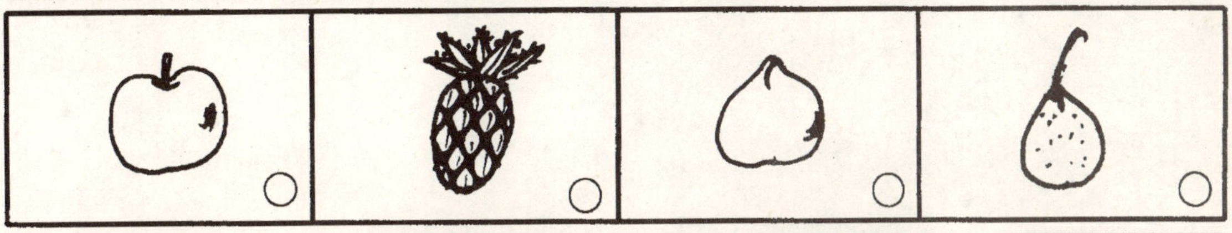

5. 说

6. 听

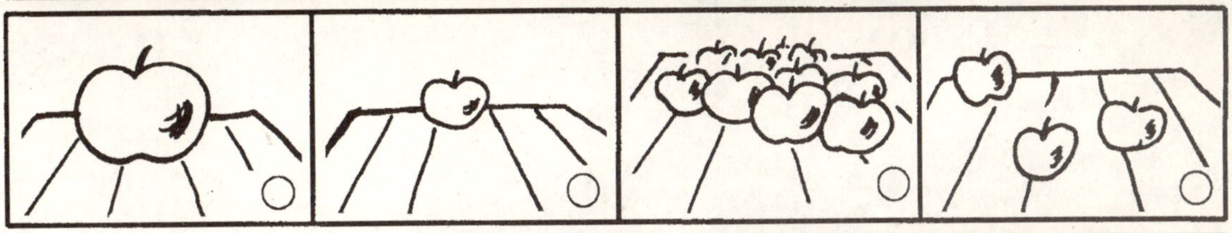

7. 说

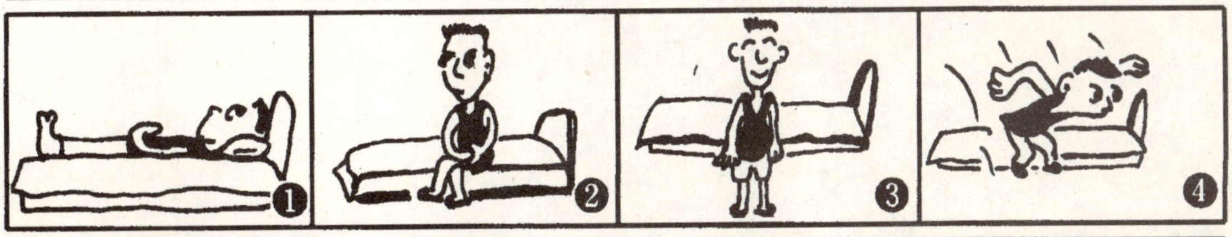

8. 听

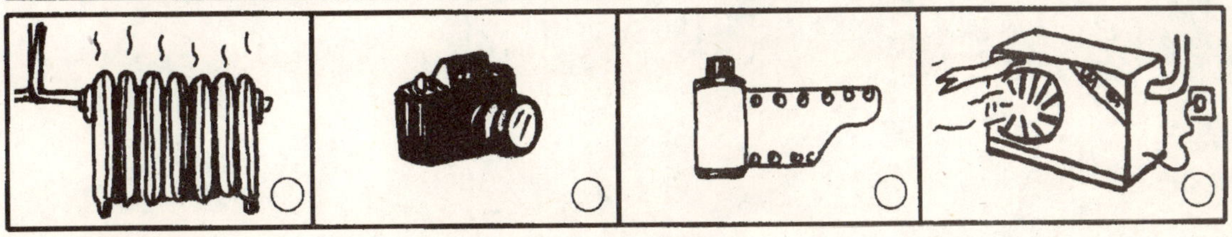

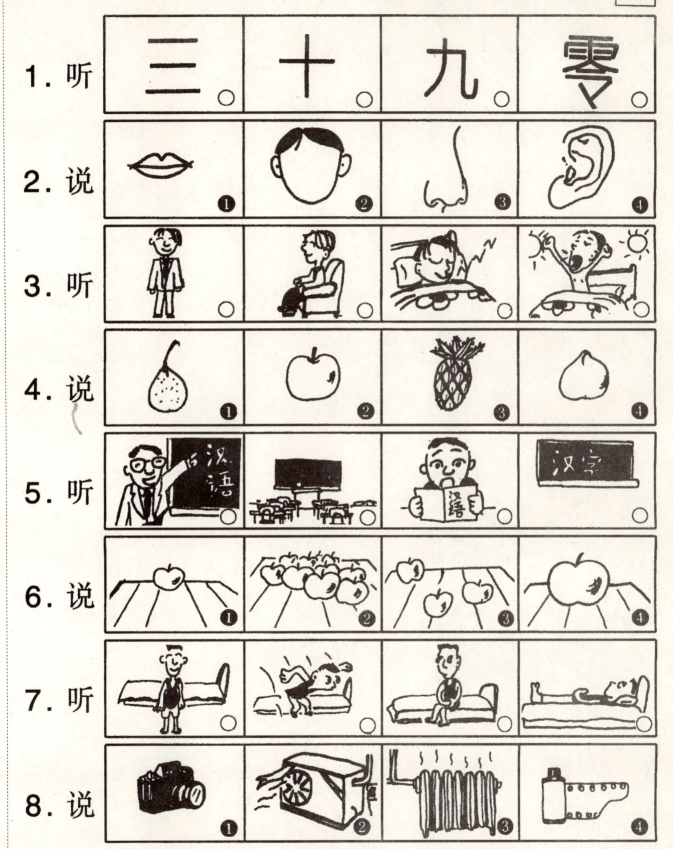

描述和排列 （一） 3A

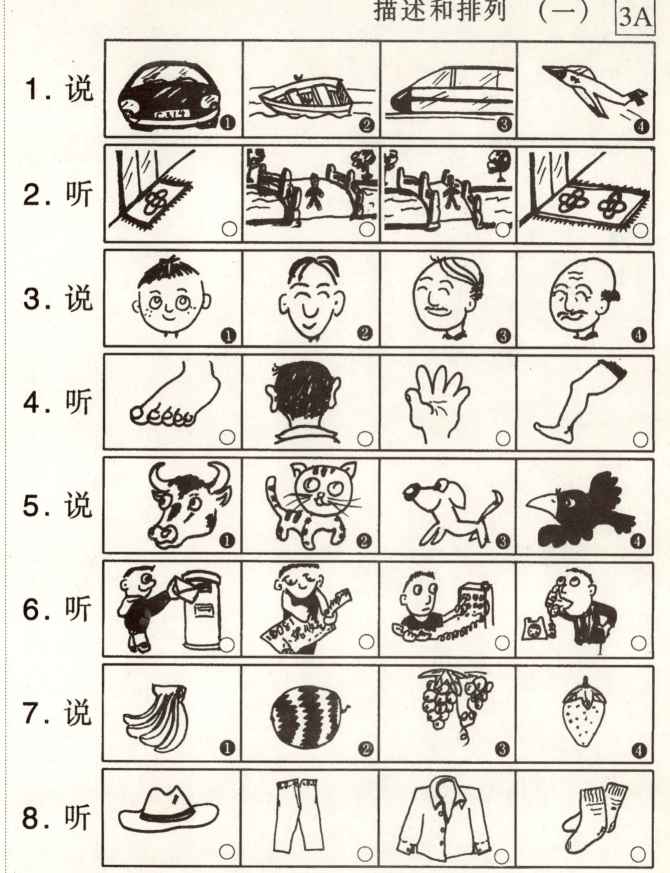

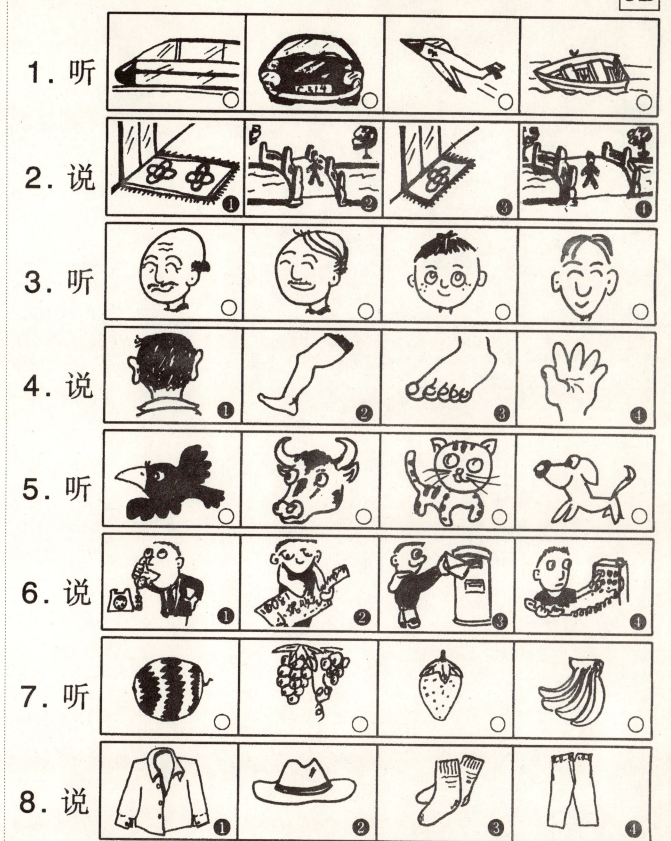

描述和排列 （一） 3B

描述和排列 （一） 4A

1. 说
2. 听
3. 说
4. 听
5. 说
6. 听
7. 说
8. 听

描述和排列 （一） 4B

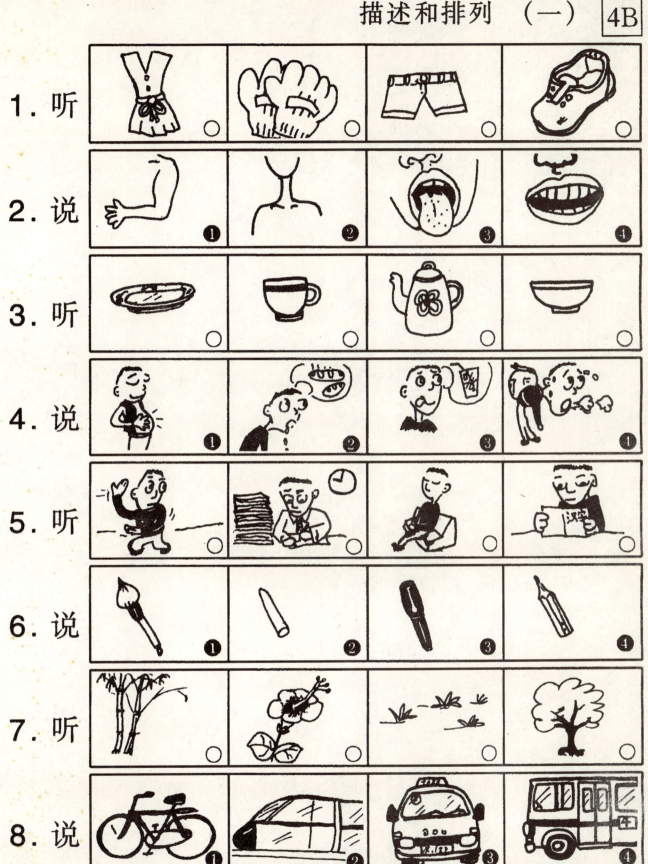

描述和排列 （一） 6A

1. 说
2. 听
3. 说
4. 听
5. 说
6. 听
7. 说
8. 听

描述和排列 （一） 6B

描述和排列 （一） 7A

1. 说

2. 听

3. 说

4. 听

5. 说

6. 听

7. 说

8. 听 九 二 五 七

描述和排列 （一）

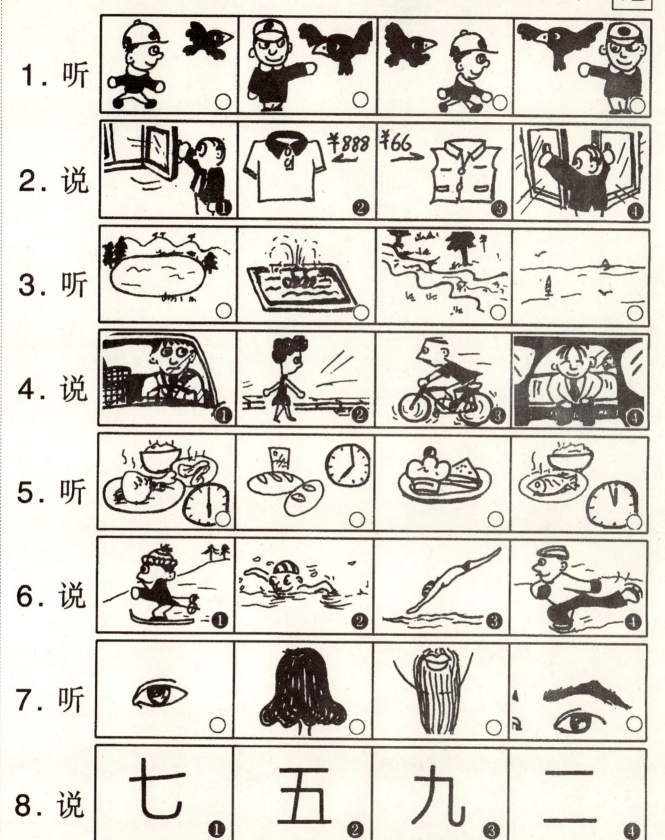

描述和排列 (一) 8A

描述和排列 （一）

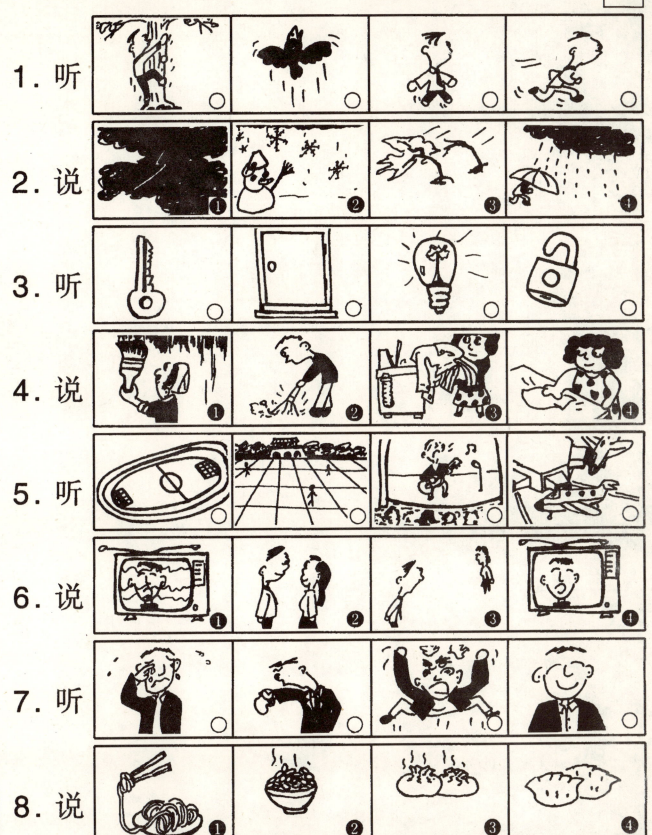

描述和排列 （一） 9A

1. 说
2. 听
3. 说
4. 听
5. 说
6. 听
7. 说
8. 听

描述和排列 （一） 9B

1. 听

2. 说

3. 听

4. 说

5. 听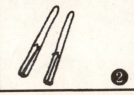

6. 说

7. 听

8. 说

描述和排列（一） 10A

1. 说
2. 听
3. 说
4. 听
5. 说
6. 听
7. 说
8. 听

描述和排列 （一） 10B

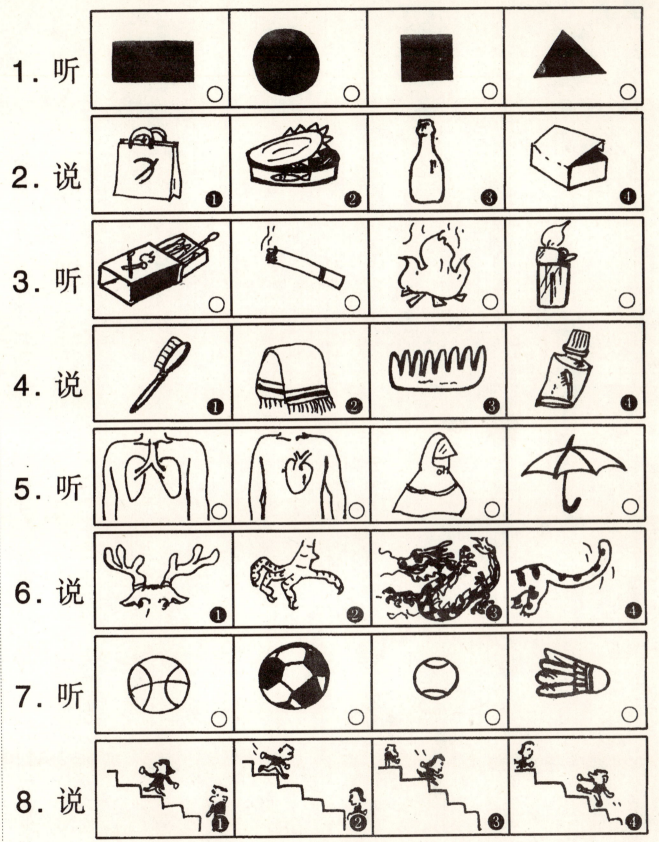

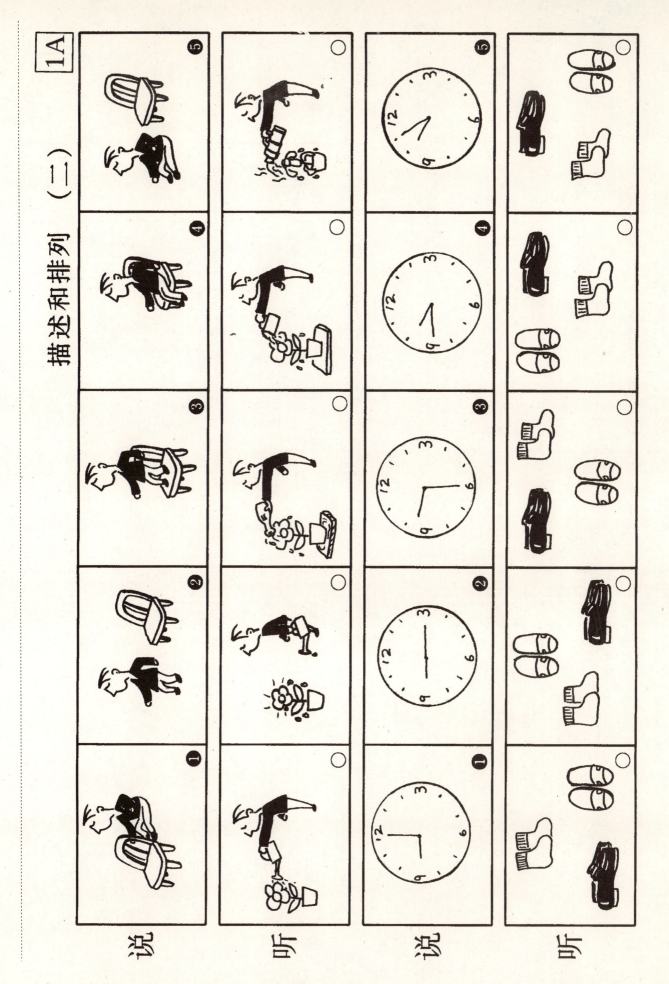

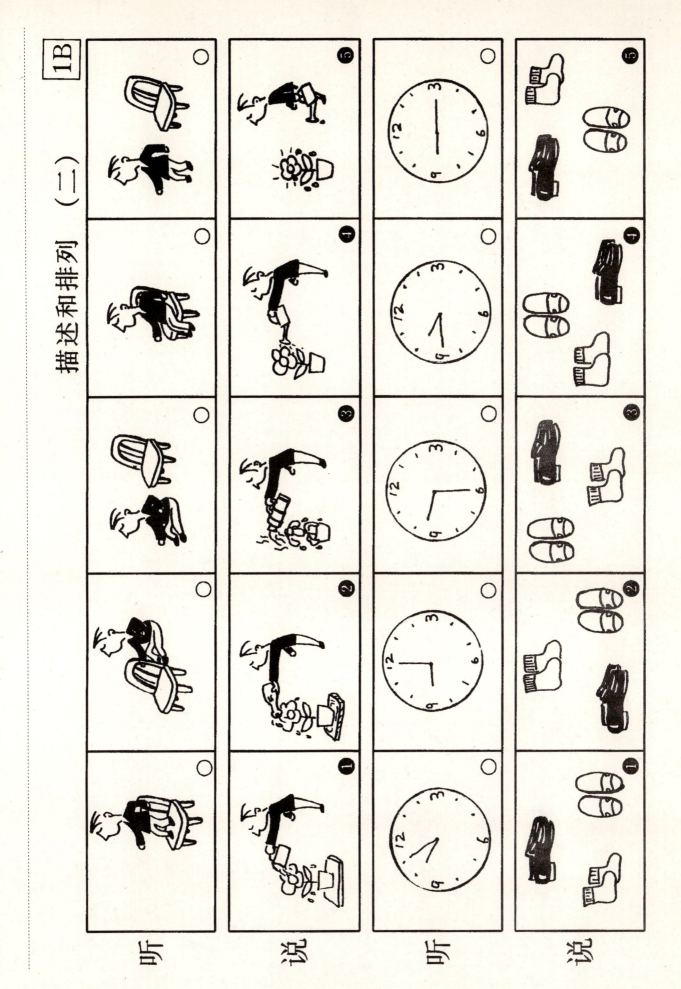

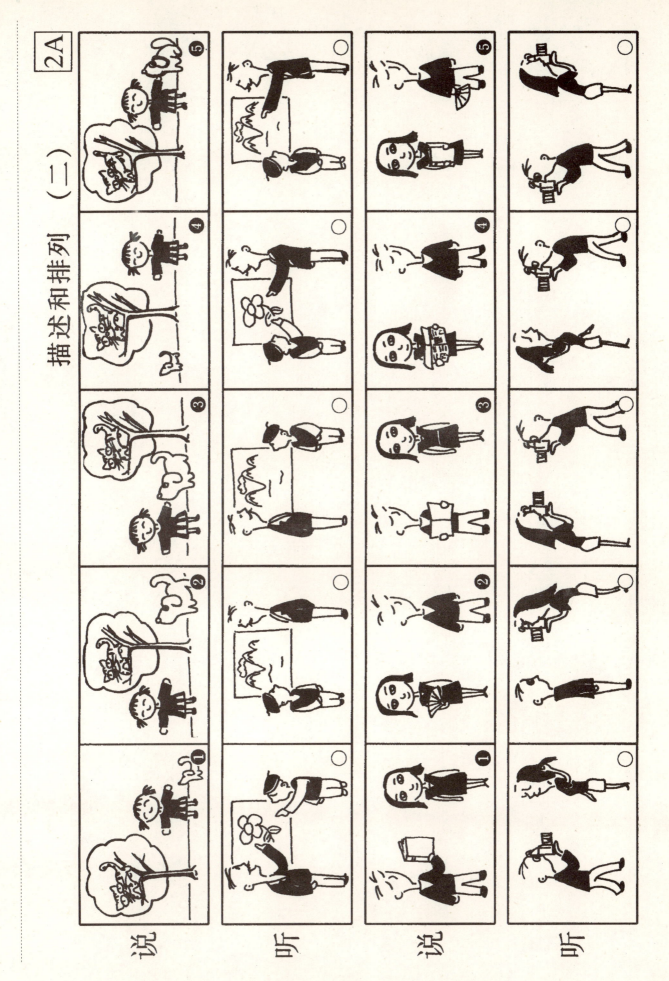

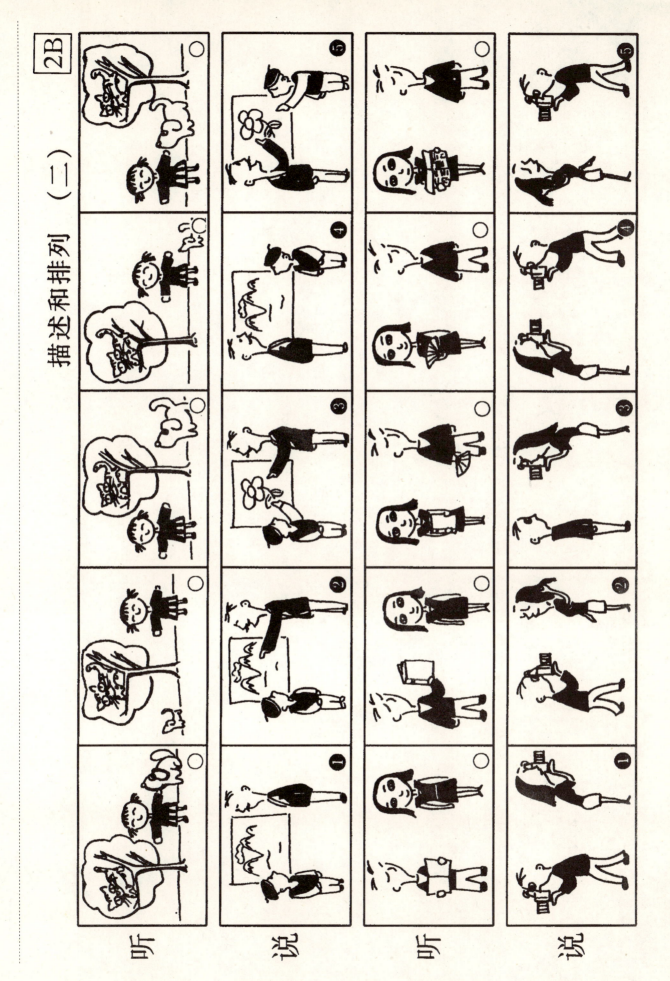

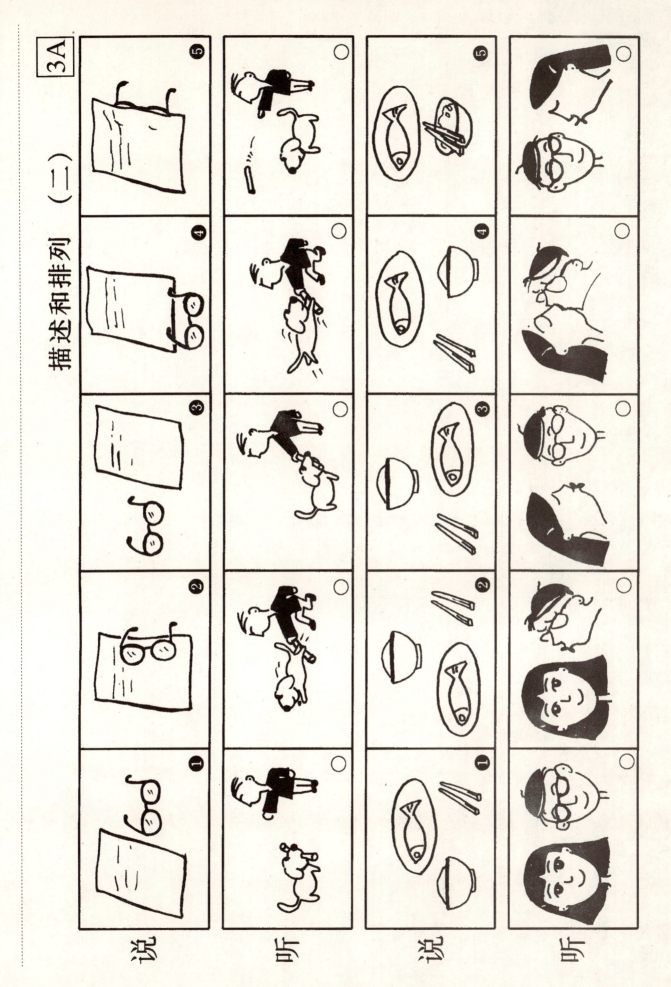

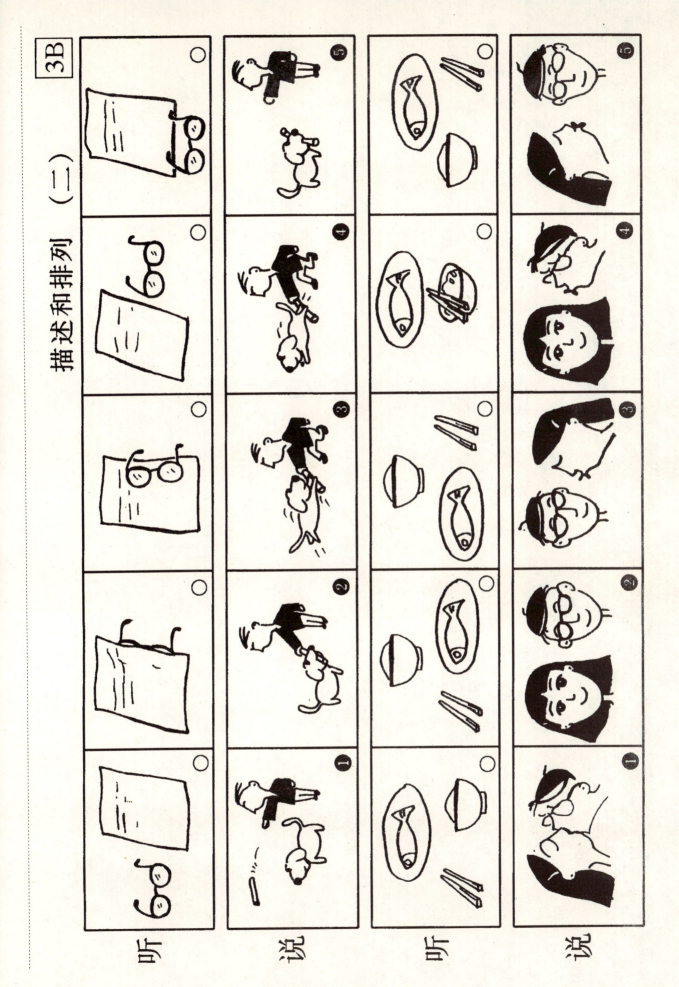

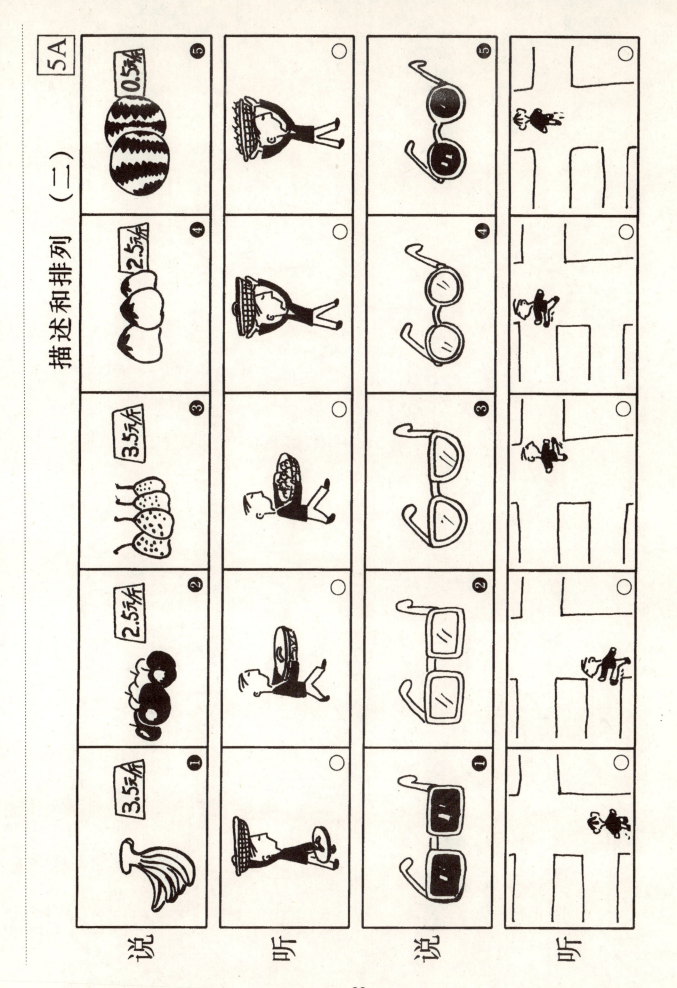

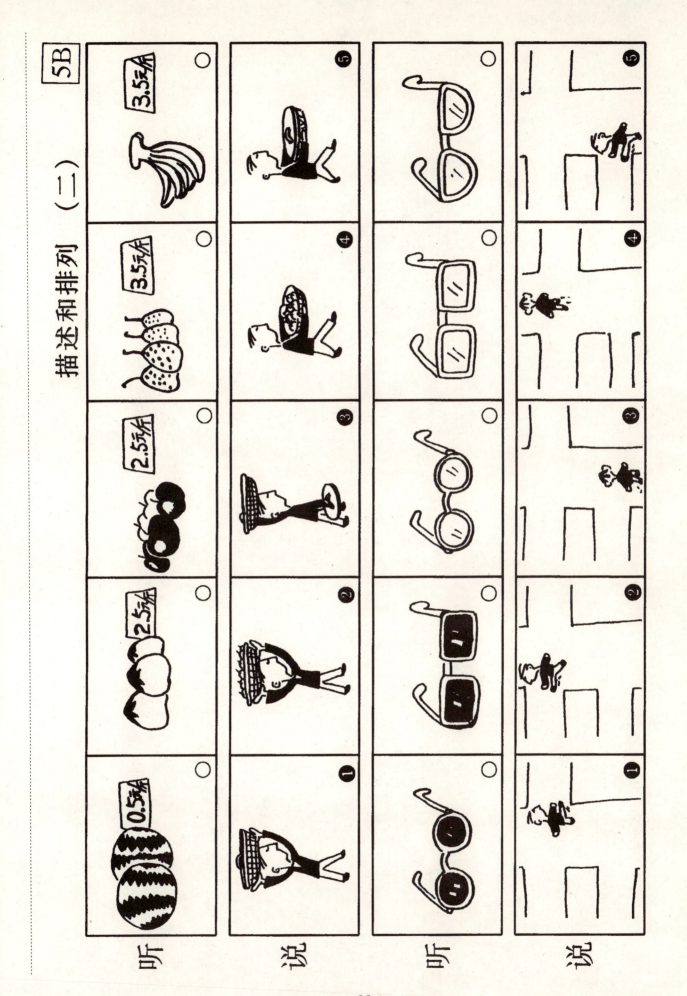

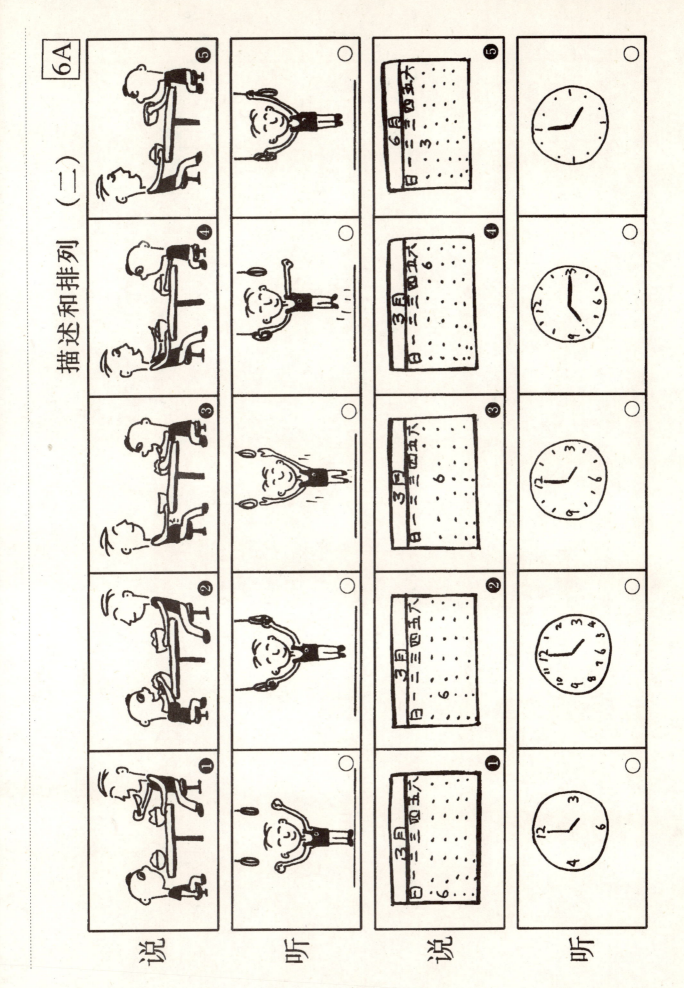

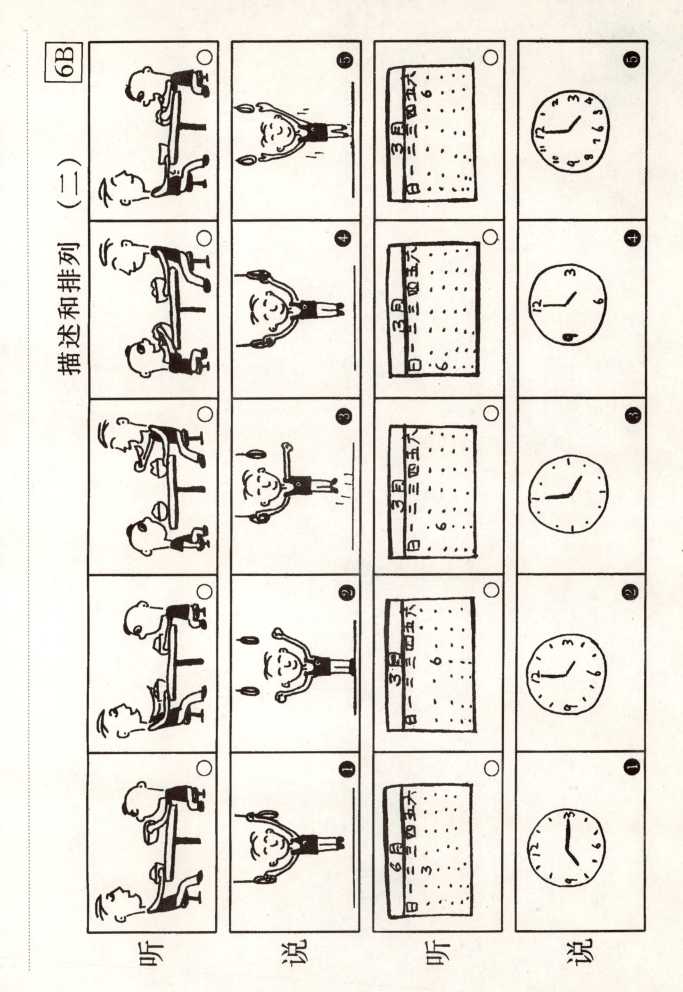

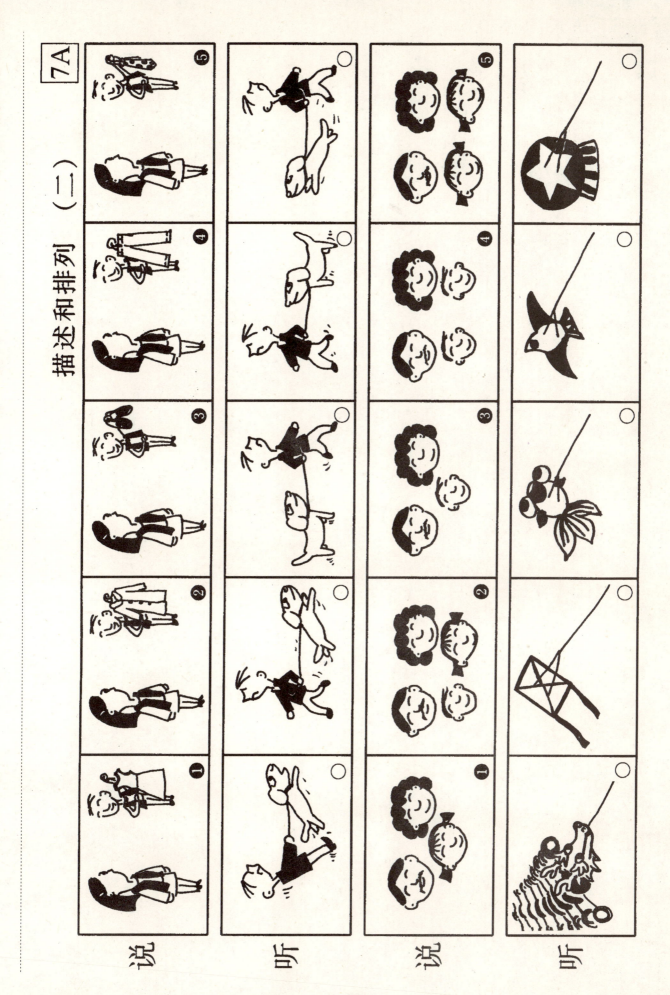

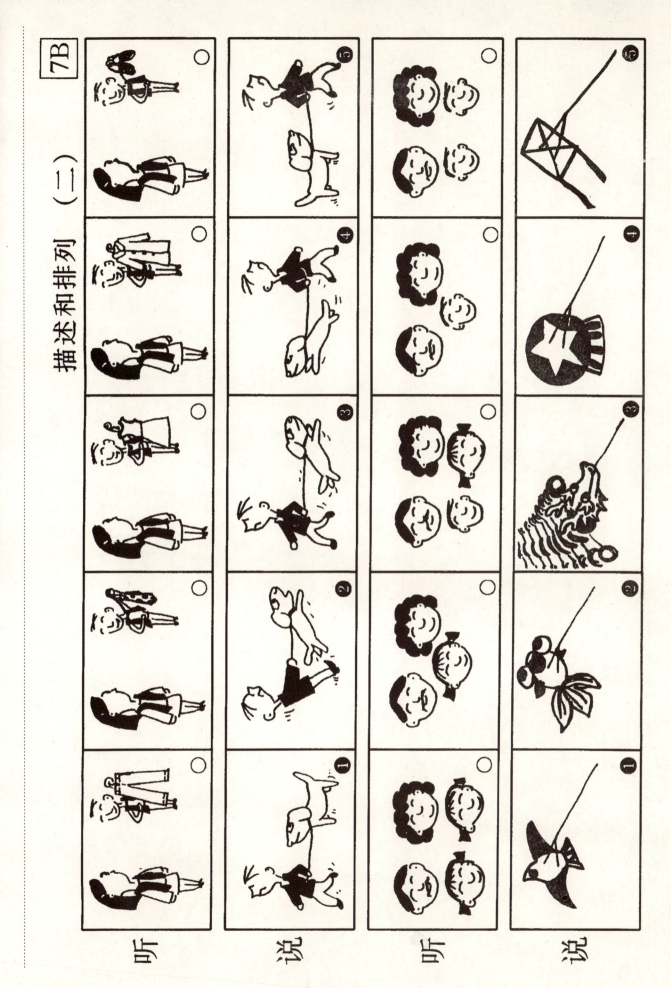

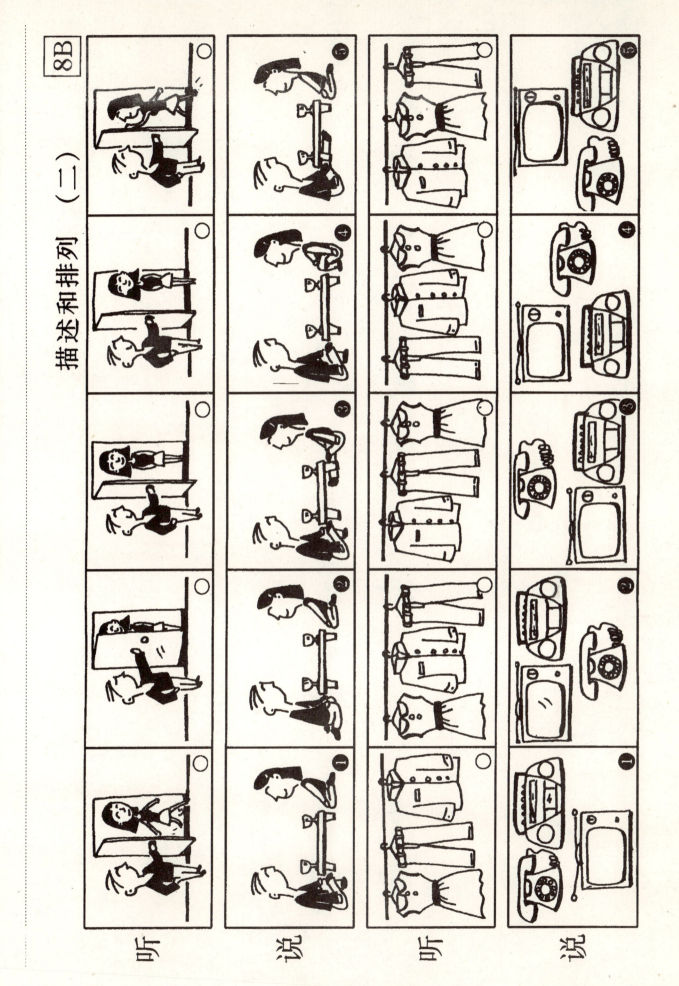

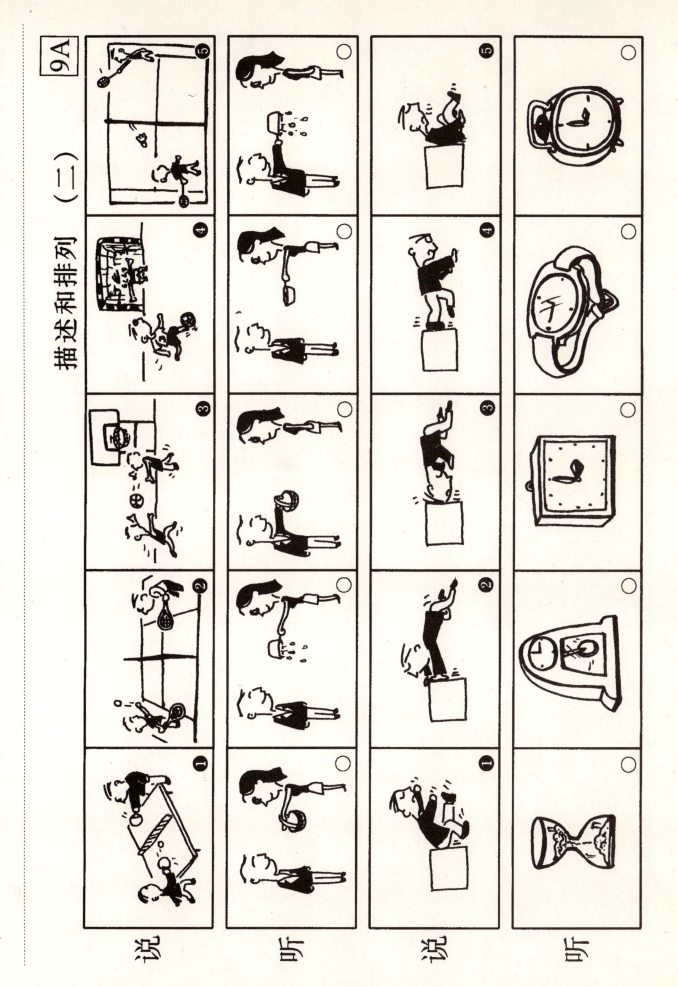

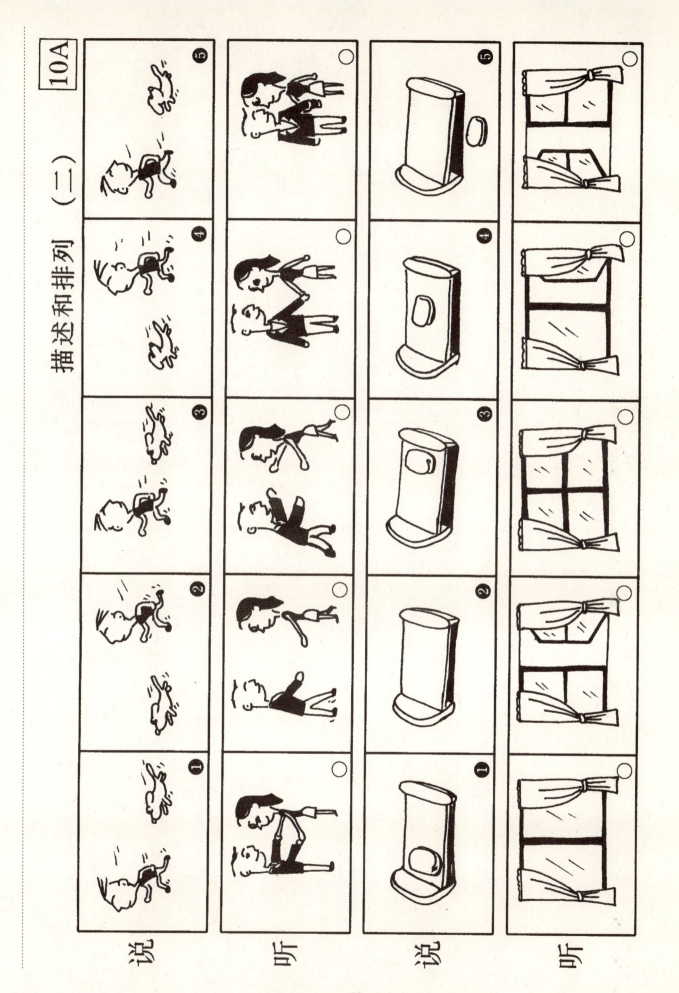

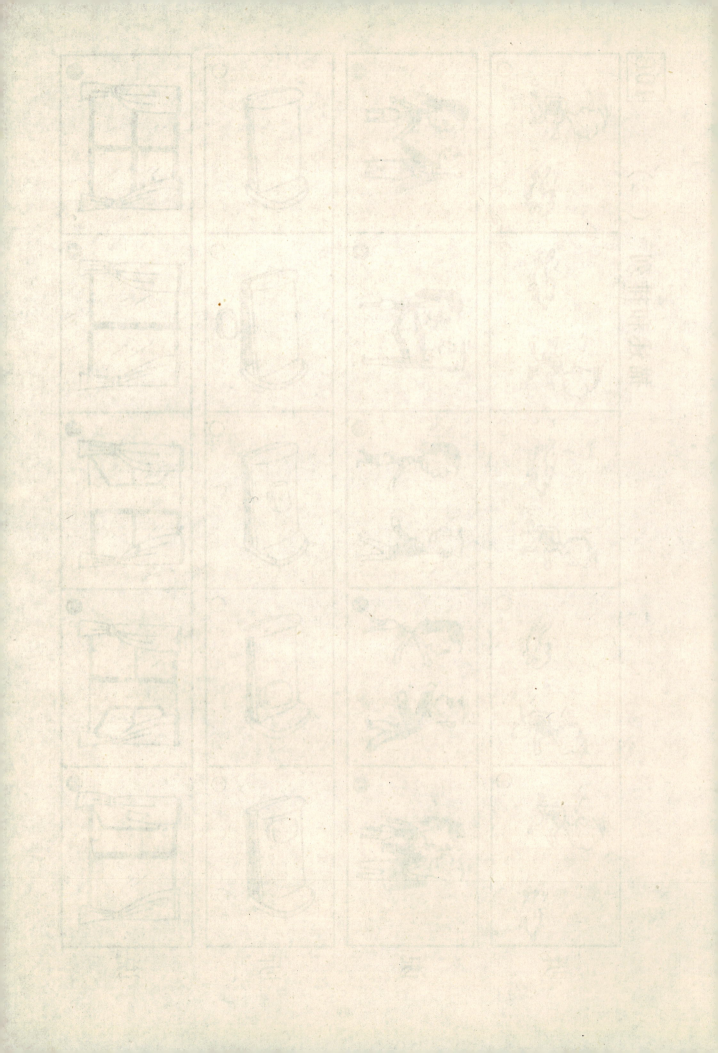

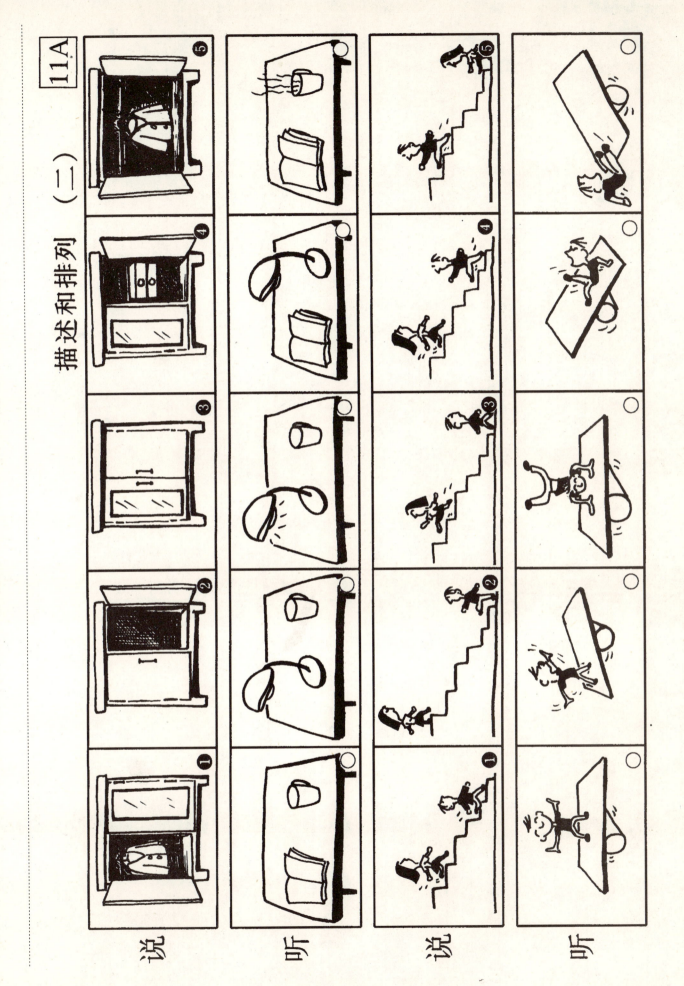

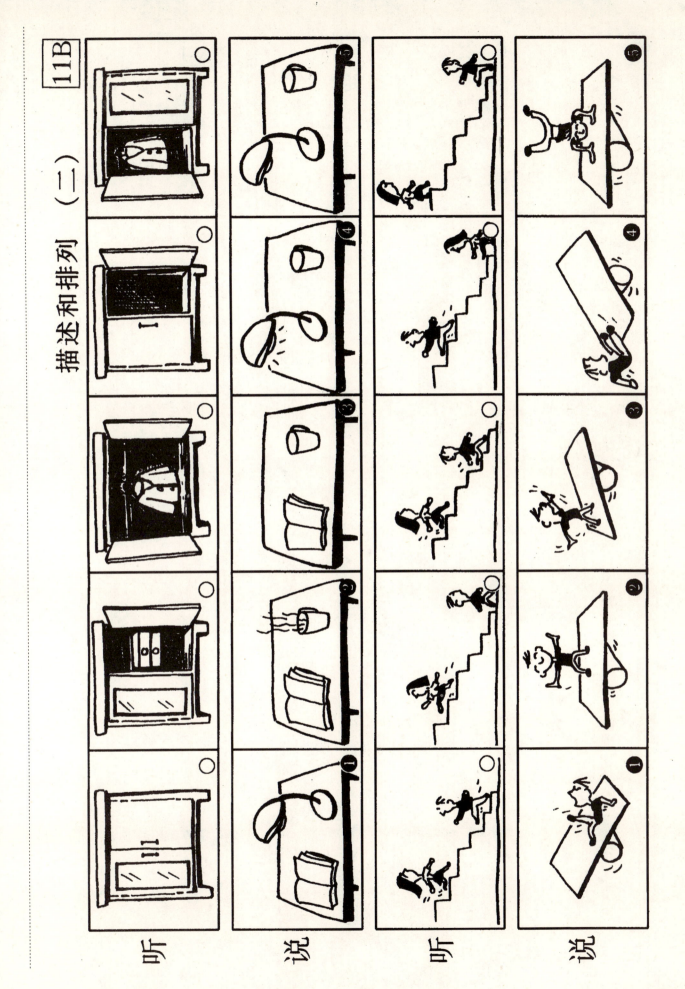

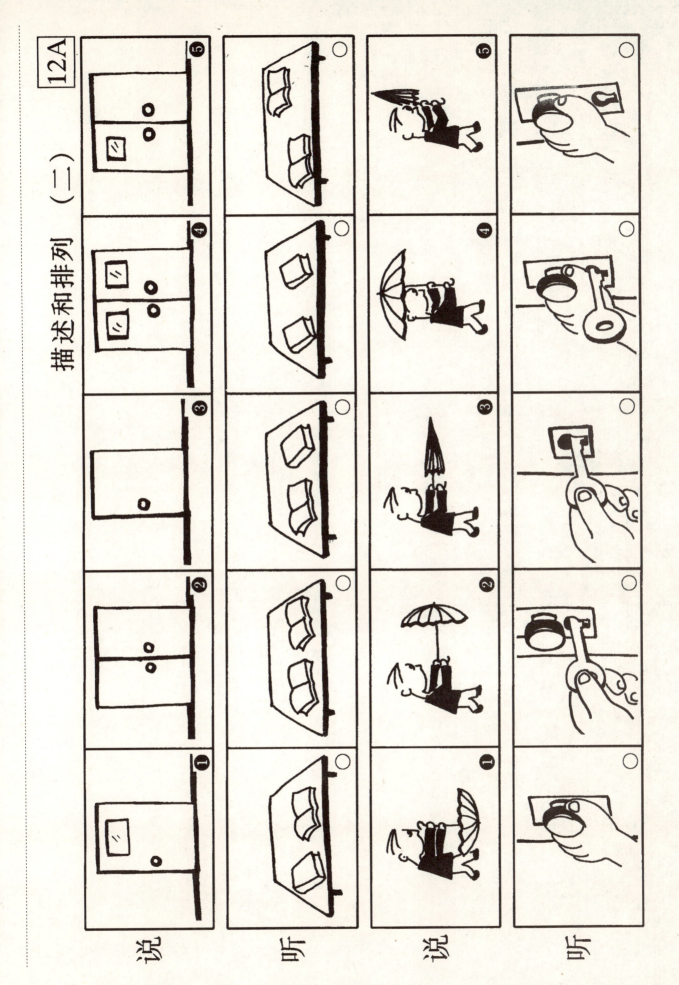

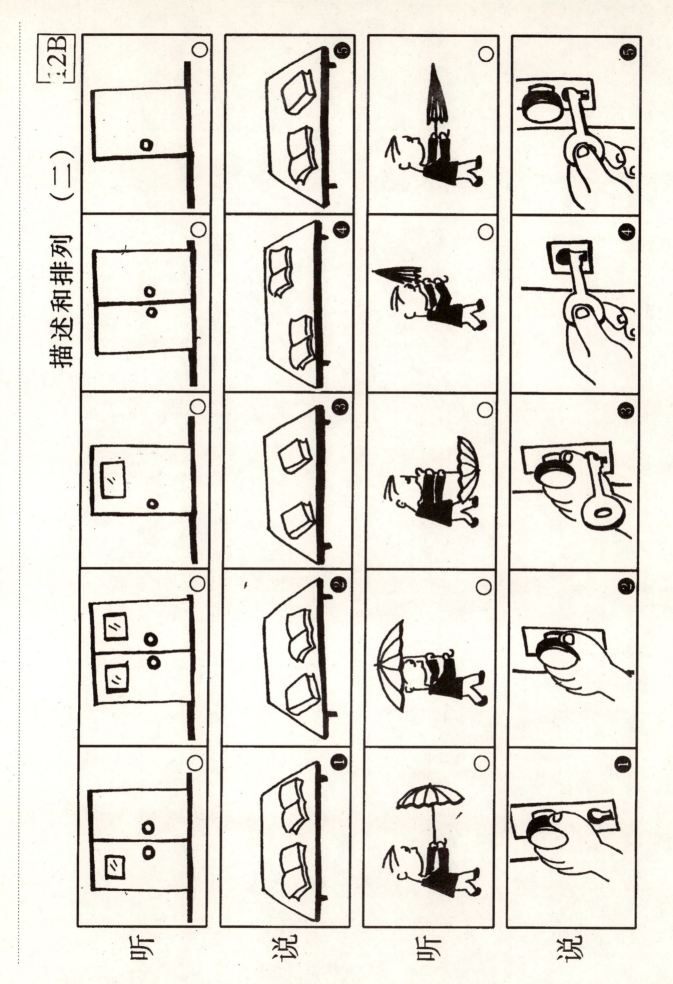

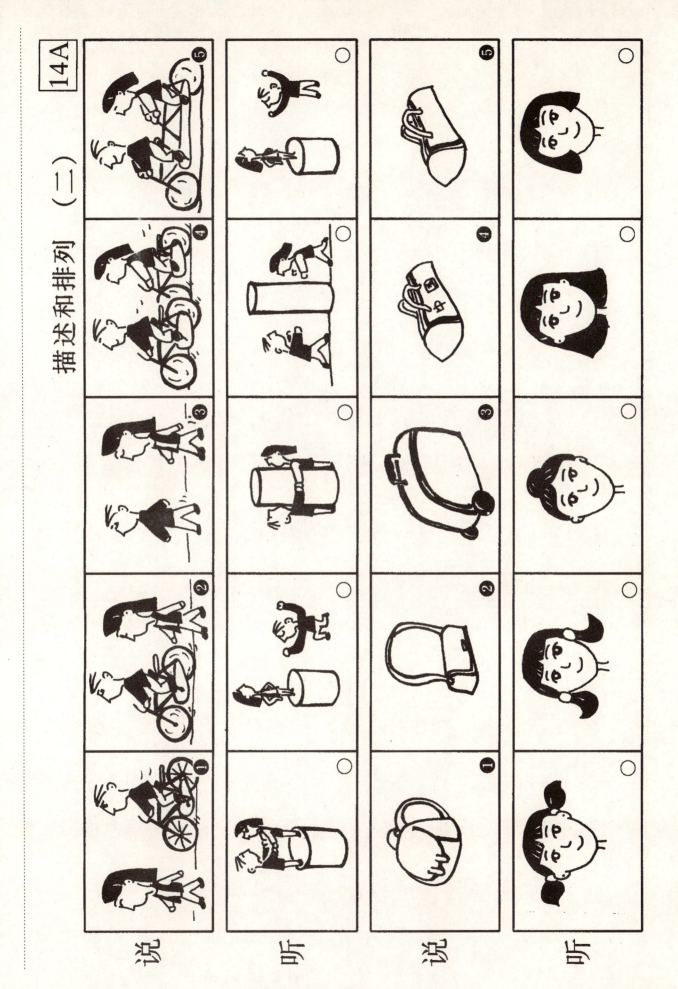

14B 描述和排列（二）

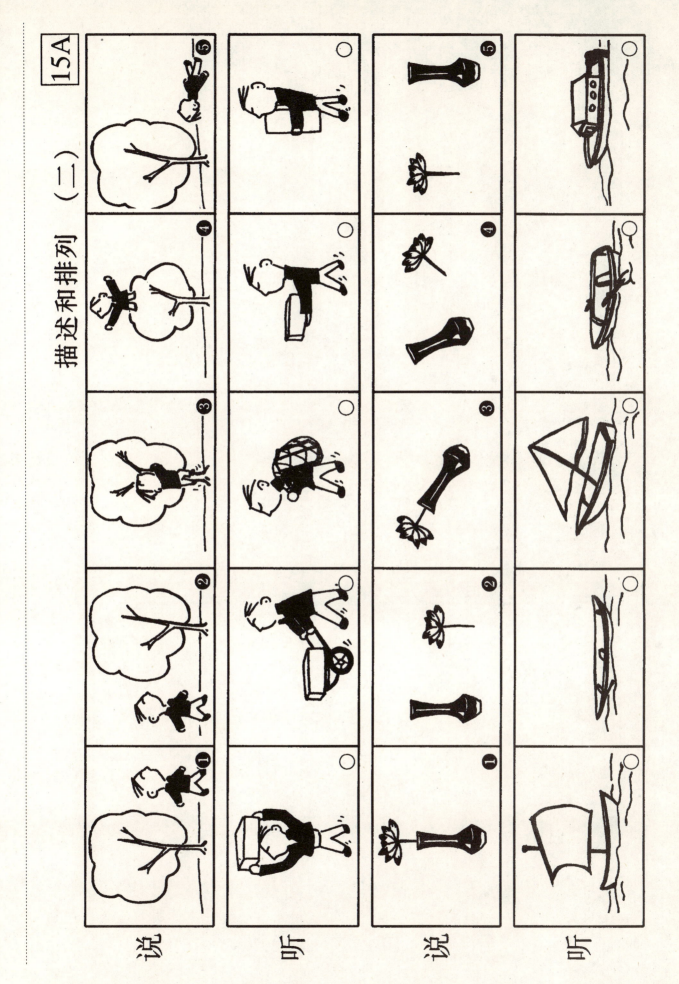

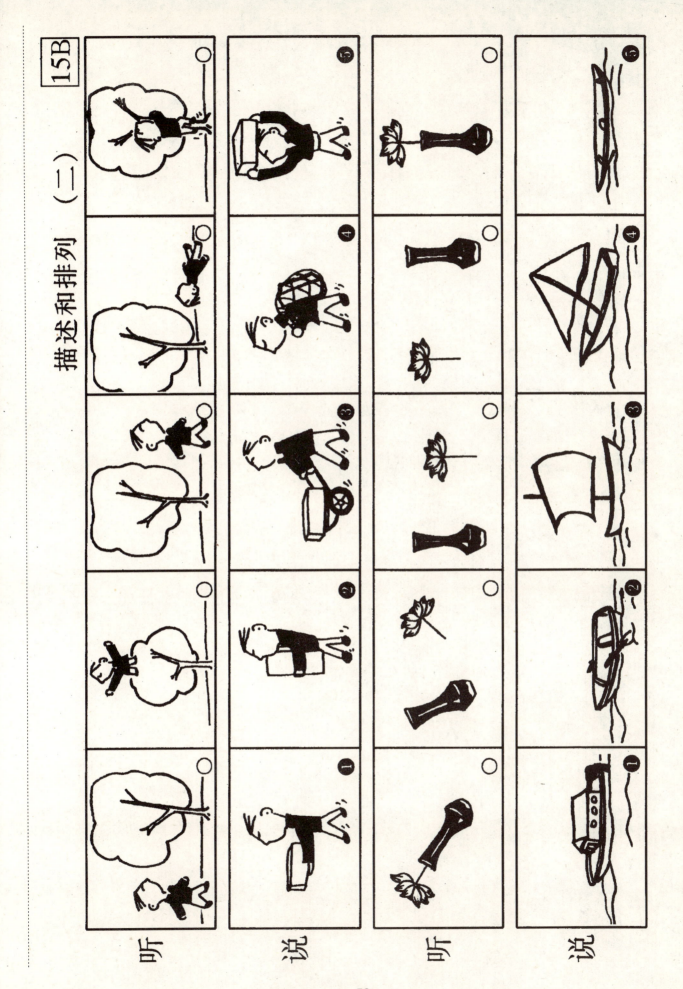

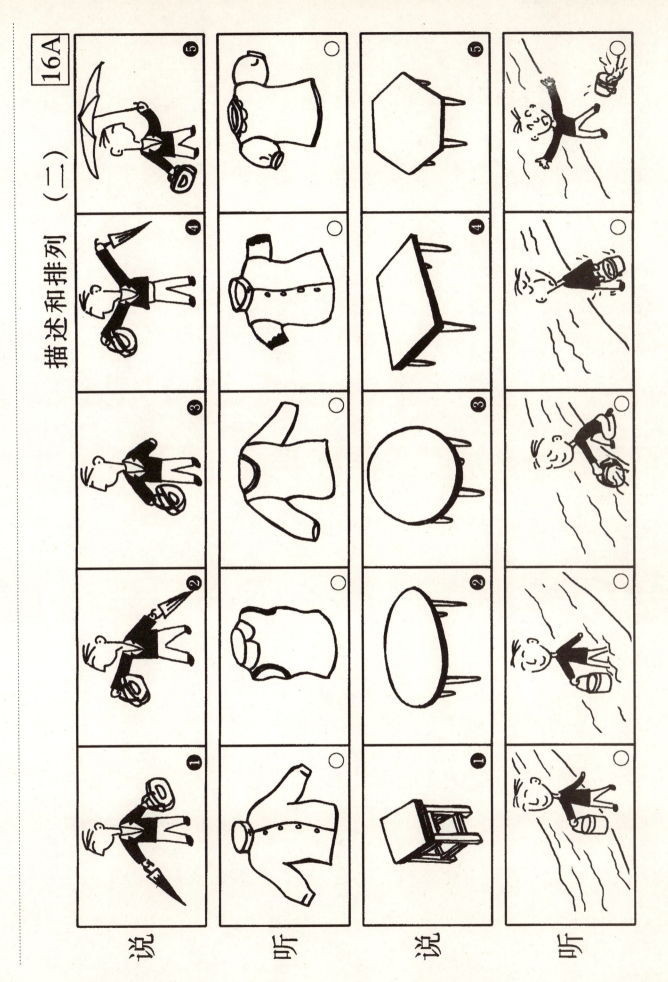

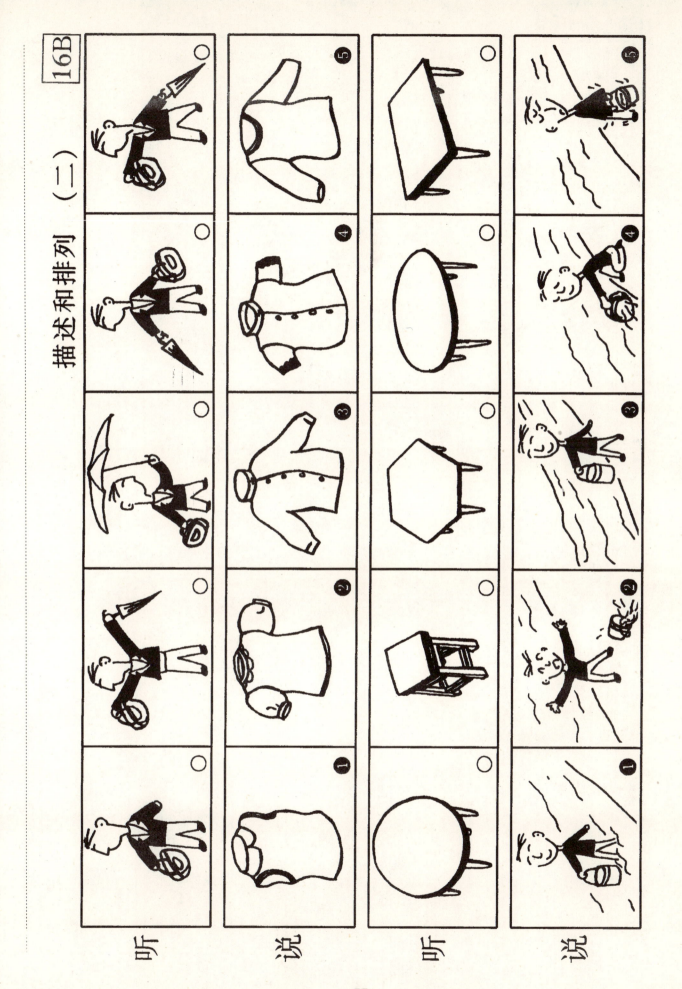

二、描述和比较

练习目的

这项练习提供 A、B 两张内容相似的图片。要求学生轮流描述和比较,找出两幅画面不同之处。

这些图片内容比较丰富,画面大部分是一种真实的情境,这就要求学生在描述时传播更多的信息,进行更细致的描述。这样自然地轮流描述与比较,使学生尽可能处于一种自由交际的状态中。这个不太复杂的交际过程,对学生来说又是一种提高语言技能的交际实践(比如,如何在交际中恰当地提出问题,如何自然地变换交际中的角色位置,等等)。

使用说明

将学生分成若干组,每组两人,分别拿着图片 A 和图片 B,互相不能看对方的图片。让学生自然地轮流描述与比较。两人的角色不固定,可以在交际过程中,选择恰当的机会自由变换。如果一方的描述不够清楚明白,另一方不能进行比较时,要马上向对方提出问题,来帮助自己进行比较,直到能比较出个结果,方可继续进行图片中别的内容的描述和比较。

注意事项

首次做这项练习时,教师应先举例说明练习方法。手举为举例而准备的图片,展示给学生,上面分别印有图片 A 和图片 B。请学生进行描述,并且同时比较其与另一幅画面内容的异同。教师在举例说明时,要简短清楚,时间最好控制在 5 分钟之内。

学生进行分组练习时,因为语言水平有高有低,练习速度有快有慢,各组自然不会同时完成。教师要善于观察学生的练习情况。当大部分学生已经完成,只有个别组的学生还没结束时,教师就要选择时机,结束这次练习。如果要大部分学生来等的话,就会使这些学生产生浪费时间的感觉,影响学生的学习积极性。如果有个别学生很快完成练习时,教师可允许他们用目的语自由交谈。

在练习过程中,如果发现有个别组只是一方一直在描述,另一方一直在比较,教师应该引导他们用自然轮流描述与比较的方式进行练习。

练习进行完后,教师最好进行一个简短的总结。常用的方法分为两步:首先教师将本次练习所使用的图片 A 和图片 B 同时展示给学生,请学生一起描述和找出两张图片内容的差别;然后,抓住图片中的一个关键内容,提出一个有趣的问题,请学生自由发表意见。这样既可以检查练习效果,给学生一个互相学习、发挥自己的机会,又可以增加练习趣味性,提高学生的学习积极性。

2. Comparing Pictures

Purpose:

In this exercise students in pairs are provided with two sheets, 'A' and 'B', both with similar (but not identical) pictures. Taking turns, the students describe and compare the pictures, trying to discover differences.

The content of the pictures is rich, and most are real-life scenes. Thus students must exchange real information, and must carry out more detailed descriptions. This kind of natural back-and-forth turn-taking and comparison lead students into fairly self-directed communication. This not-so-complicated interaction provides a way to practise and increase communicative skills (for example, how to present questions during an interaction, how to exchange roles during an interaction, etc.).

Procedure:

Separate the students into groups, two people per group, one person with sheet A and the other with sheet B. Each person cannot look directly at the other person's sheet. The students describe and compare in natural turns. The roles of each person are not set, and can change freely during the interaction at the appropriate times. If one person's description is not clear enough, and the other person is unable to continue comparing, then that person should immediately ask for clarification from the person currently describing to help carry out the comparison, until a result is obtained and the next point can be compared.

Important Points:

The first time through this exercise the instructor should go through an example trial run, using the provided example sheet (marked for both A and B roles on a single sheet), to show how the exercise should be carried out. The teacher should hold the example sheet before the class, and ask the students to describe, while at the same time comparing differences between A and B. The trial run should be simple and clear, and should be kept under five minutes.

Because of differences in target language level within a given group, some groups will progress quickly, and some slowly, and will finish the exercise at different times. The instructor should monitor the progress of the exercise closely, and end the exercise when most groups have finished, and maybe just one or two groups have not quite finished. If most groups have to wait too long, they will feel that they are wasting time and this will affect the students' attitudes towards the exercise. If a few students finish very early, they can be allowed to chat in the target language.

During the exercise if there are some groups that have one person continually describing, and the other comparing, without changing roles, then the instructor should help them to a more natural turn-taking mode of carrying out the exercise.

After completion, the instructor should carry out a short summary exercise. Usually this contains two steps. First, the instructor can take sheets A and B and show them to the class and have them describe and compare. Afterwards, the instructor can pick a significant item or two from the pictures and bring up some interesting questions, and have the students give their opinions. This allows the instructor to check up on the exercise results, gives students an opportunity to learn from each other, and allows them to express themselves. It also makes the exercise more interesting, and increases the degree of student participation.

描述和比较 [举例]

描述和比较 1A

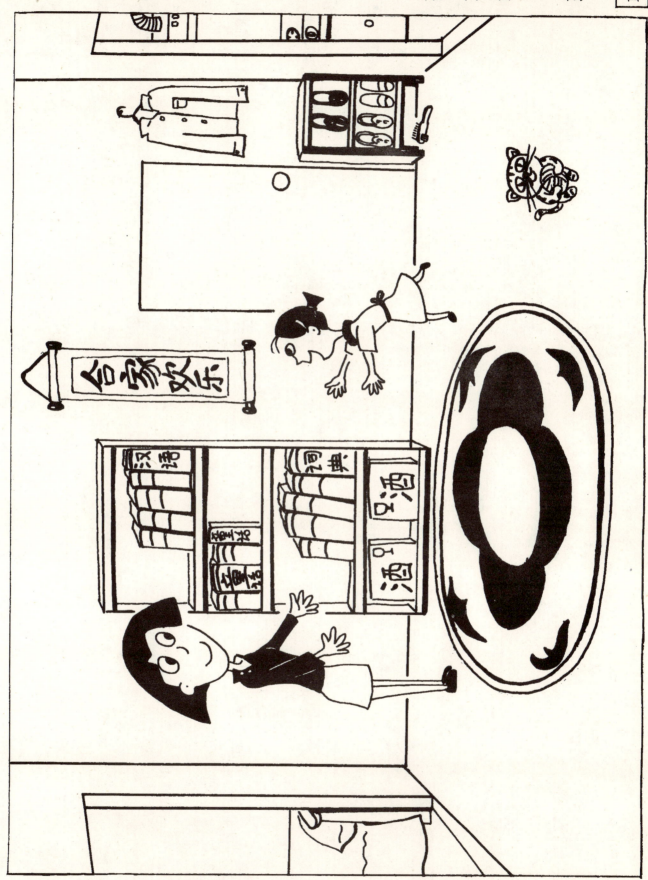

描述和比较 1B

描述和比较 2A

描述和比较

2 B

请勿吸烟

你们好吗
老师好吗
学汉语

描述和比较 3A

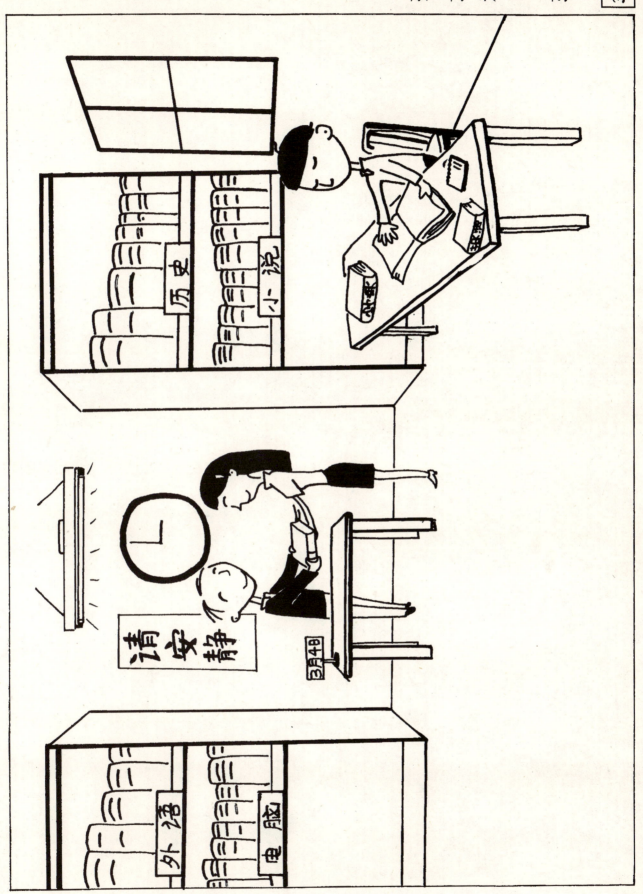

描述和比较 3B

描述和比较 4A

描述和比较 4B

描述和比较 5A

描述和比较

描述和比较 6A

描述和比较

描述和比较

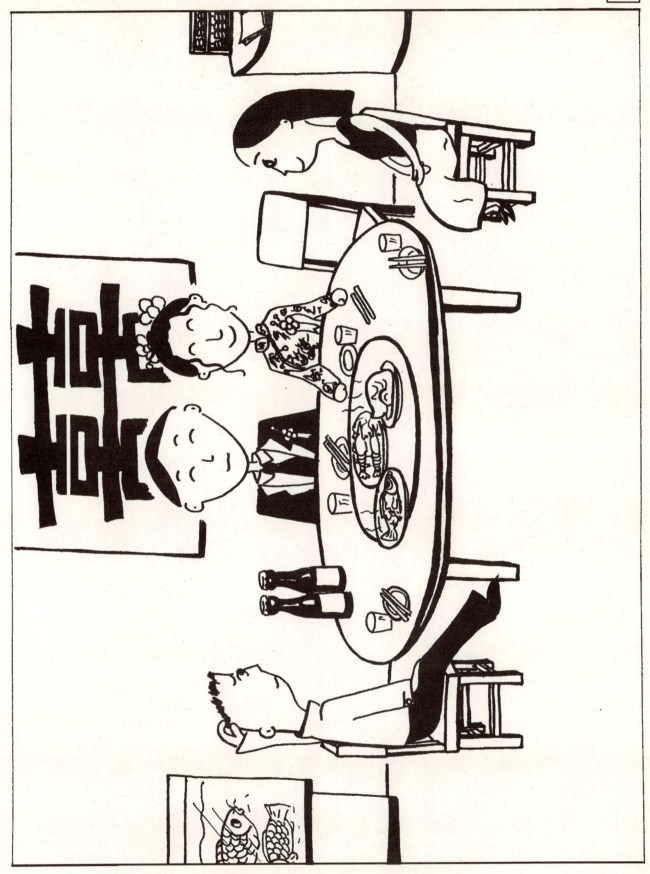

描述和比较 7B

描述和比较 8A

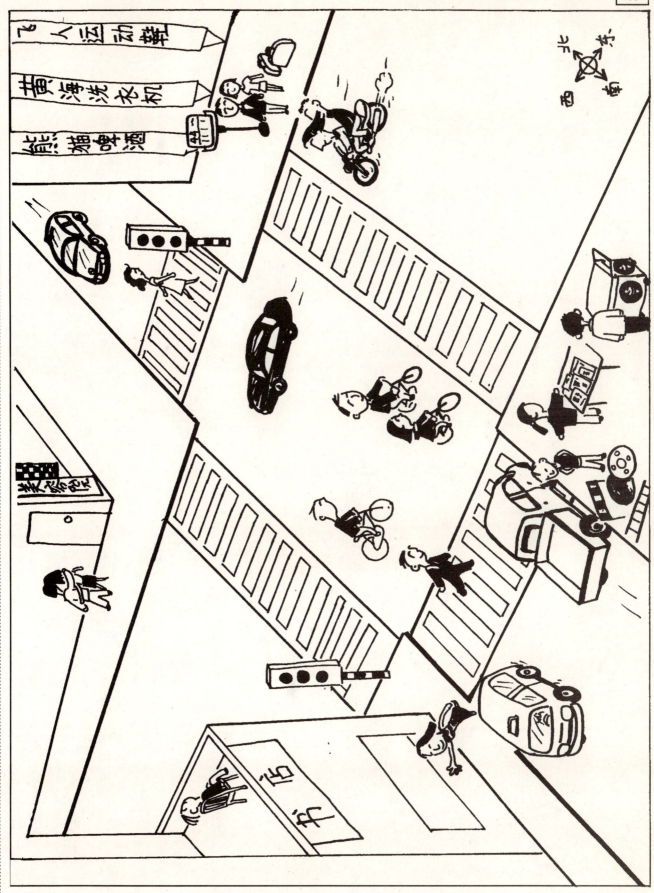

描述和比较 8 B

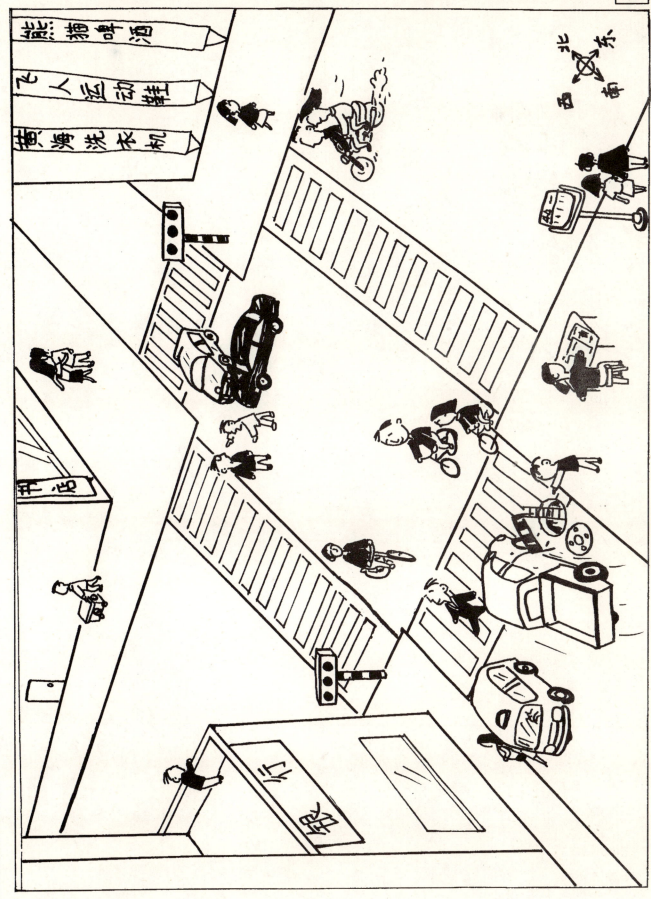

描述和比较 9A

描述和比较 9B

描述和比较

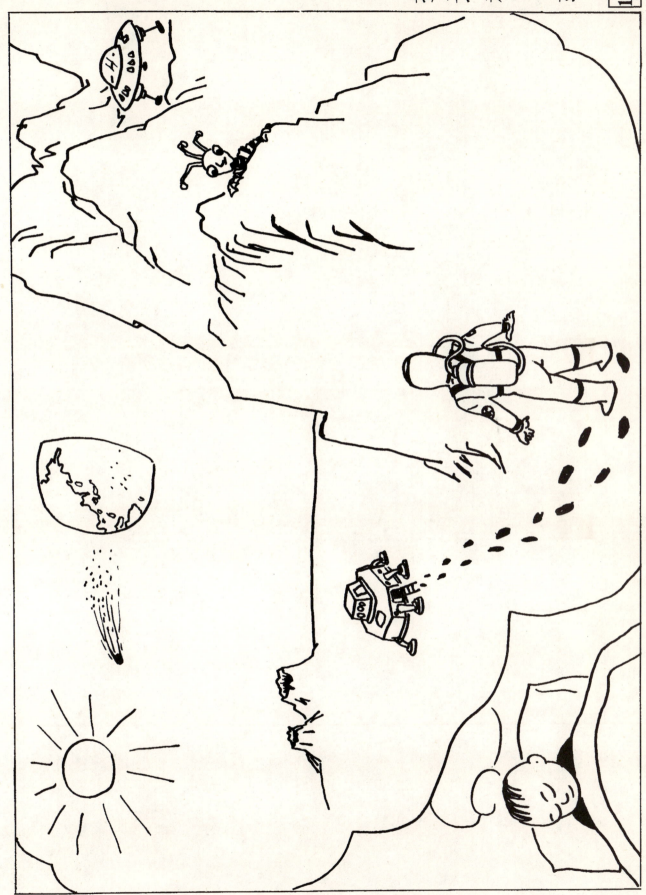

描述和比较 10 B

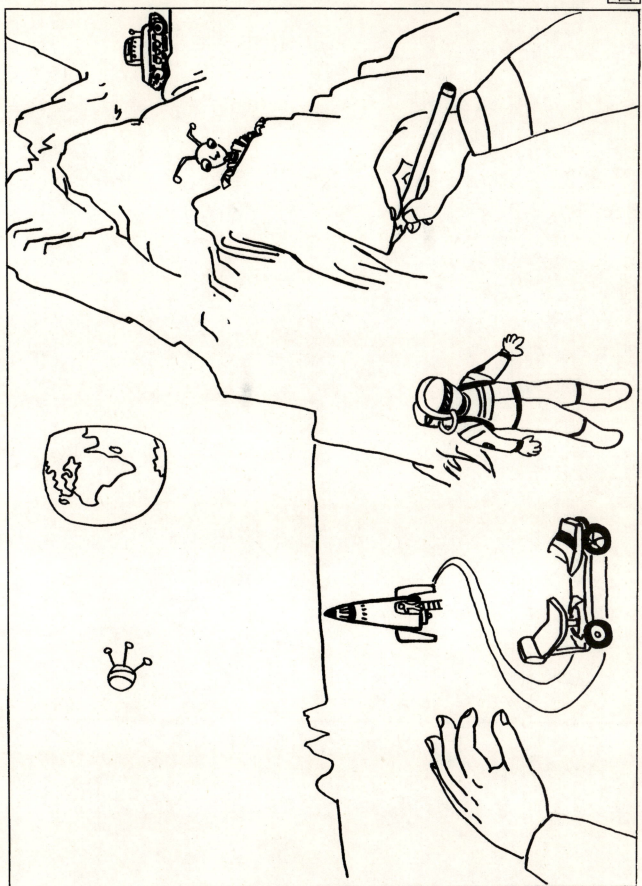

· 78 ·

三、描述和绘画

练习目的

　　这项练习提供一幅具有丰富内容的图片,要求学生一人描述,另一人绘画。在描述和绘画时,绘画者可以根据需要随时提问。描述者应该一边描述,一边监督绘画效果。在这个交际过程中,使学生学会如何在交际时尽可能完整准确地发出信息,以及如何在交际中更快更准地获得自己所需的信息。

使用说明

　　将学生分成若干组,每组两人。一人为描述者,手拿教师所给的图片,另一人为绘画者,准备好一张绘画用的纸。

　　描述者不能让绘画者看手中的图片,只是向绘画者详细而有条理地描述手中图片的内容,同时监督绘画的准确性并及时指点。描述者必须充分考虑到画面上各种信息的相互关系(如物体位置、人物关系,等等)及画面细节。作为一种信息的反馈,绘画者要在纸上尽可能准确地画出来。如果描述不够准确清楚,或者因理解障碍而不能准确地画出来时,绘画者就要向描述者提出问题,来帮助自己完成这幅图画。

　　当绘画者根据描述者的描述完成这幅图画后,描述者将手中的图片向绘画者展示,两人共同比较两张图片的异同。

注意事项

　　首次做这项练习时,教师应该先向学生简单介绍练习方法,不用详细地举例说明。

　　练习完后,教师最好进行一个简短的总结。自由选择几幅绘画者的图片向全体学生展示,请学生从正确性和画面的完整性简要评论这些图片。最后,教师可结合图片内容提出一两个有趣的问题,请学生充分发挥想像力,自由回答。

3. Drawing a Picture

Purpose:

In this exercise pairs of students are provided with a picture. One student describes the picture and the other draws it out based on the first person's description. During this time of description and drawing, the person drawing can ask clarification questions at any time. The person describing monitors the drawing process as he or she is decribing the picture to insure accuracy. During this communicative process students learn how to most accurately and completely pass information, and how, during communication, to quickly and accurately get needed information.

Procedure:

Separate the students into groups, two people per group. The person who will describe has the picture provided by the instructor, and the person who will draw has a blank sheet of paper.

The person describing must not let the person drawing see the picture in his or her hand, but should instead clearly describe the contents of the picture in detail. That person should also monitor the drawing, and point out corrections or make suggestions in a timely fashion as needed. The person describing should carefully consider the organization of elements in the picture (for example, the locations of items, relationships between people, etc.), and general picture details as he or she describes it. In response, the person drawing should do the best to accurately draw out the picture. If the description is not clear enough, or if there is any problem in understanding, then the person drawing should ask questions to make it possible to finish the picture.

When the drawing is finished, the person describing can then show the original picture, and the two people can compare the pictures.

Important Points:

The first time through this exercise the instructor should explain how to carry it out in a simple fashion. There is no need for an elaborate example trial run.

After the exercise the instructor should perform a short group summary exercise. The instructor can select a few student drawings and show them to the whole class, and ask for student comments on the accuracy of the drawings. After that, the instructor can pose questions on a couple of interesting points concerning the content of the original picture and have the students answer freely based on their own imagination.

描述和绘画 1、2

描述和绘画 3、4

③

④

· 83 ·

描述和绘画 5、6

描述和绘画　7、8

描述和绘画 9、10

描述和绘画 11、12

四、看图说话

练习目的

这项练习提供几幅具有连续性情节的画面。要求学生对画面所提供的信息进行充分的讨论,根据画面内容描述一个完整的故事。学生在讨论中要全面考虑到画面信息的连续性、条理性,在自己现有的目的语水平上,利用自己掌握了的词汇和语法规则,将所要传播的信息进行归纳和总结,使所描述的故事不但详细完整,而且条理清晰。

使用说明

将学生分成若干组,每组二至四人,教师将图片发给每个组。首先给学生几分钟准备时间,请每个组的学生一起讨论画面的内容,做好发言的准备。发言的方式有两种,教师可自由决定:一种是每个组自己推举一个代表进行发言,另一种是每个组的学生分别描述画面中的一部分内容。

注意事项

教师可自由选用画面相同的或画面不同的图片,两种方式各有侧重:

(1)每个组用画面相同的图片,可以使整个课堂练习成为一个整体,后发言的组可以不断从前边的组的发言中获得帮助(比如生词、句子、表达方式,等等),不断补充到自己的发言中去,自我完善。

(2)每个组用画面不同的图片,可以激发学生的练习积极性。为了表现出色,每个组都会竭尽全力准备他们的发言,而且每个组的发言内容都不同,使学生们在课堂上获得的语言信息量大大增加,有助于学生自始至终对练习保持浓厚兴趣。

首次做这项练习时,教师应先举例说明练习方法,手举那张为举例而准备的图片,向学生展示,与学生共同讨论画面内容,有条理地描述出一个完整的故事,使学生明白此项练习的要求。

课堂练习结束后,教师可以给学生布置一个课外作业,将练习变为看图写话。学生要将写好的文章交给教师,教师批改后再发给学生。这样可以使教师全面了解每个学生的练习情况,也使听、说、读、写四种技能训练较好地结合,有助于学生全面提高语言水平。

4. Telling a Story

Purpose:

In this exercise students in small groups are provided with a series of pictures on a single sheet of paper. Through thorough discussion the students create a complete story based on the plot and theme portrayed in the pictures. During discussion students consider all aspects of the information portrayed in the pictures, including connectedness and order, and using the target language skills at whatever level of mastery attained, in vocabulary, grammar, etc., take the information contained in the pictures and express a complete and reasonable story.

Procedure:

Separate the students into groups, two to four people per group. After passing out the papers, one per group, have each group of students spend several minutes discussing the contents of the pictures, create a single complete story together, and get ready to present their story to the class. During presentations the instructor can choose to select a single person from each group to speak, or can have each member speak a portion of the story.

After each presentation, if there are any concerns with the story presented, or if there are details that were missed, the listeners can express questions to the speakers, and the speakers will need to try to explain or justify their understanding of the story portrayed in the pictures.

Important Points:

The instructor may choose to either give all the groups the same picture, or give a different picture to each group. Each way has its own emphasis:

1) By using the same picture for each group, the whole classroom exercise is more unified. Groups that present later can continually get help by watching the earlier groups present (for example in vocabulary, sentence types, presentation method, etc.), and thus be able to continually improve their own up-coming presentations.

2) By using different pictures for each group, interest is stimulated. In order to present their own story well, each group will work diligently to prepare. Additionally, since the content is different for each group, the amount of language information in the classroom is increased. This all helps to ensure interest in the exercise from beginning to end.

The first time through this exercise the instructor should make an example trial run, using the provided example sheet, to show how the exercise should be carried out. The teacher should hold the example sheet before the class, discuss the content together with the students, and together create a reasonable story. This will help to ensure that students understand the requirements of the exercise.

After the exercise the instructor may set up an out-of-class homework by requiring students to write out a story based on the pictures, to be turned in to the teacher, and later returned to the student. In this way the teacher can better understand each student's circumstances, and make this exercise into a general unified practice of the four major skills of listening, speaking, reading, and writing, and thus helping to raise the student's overall level in the target language.

看图说话 1

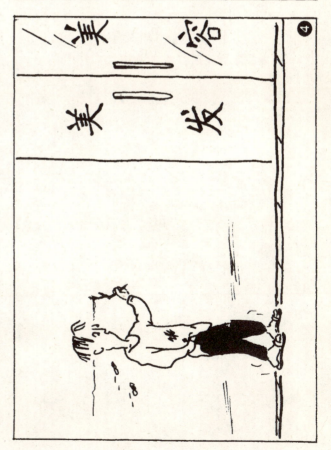

看图说话 2

看图说话 3

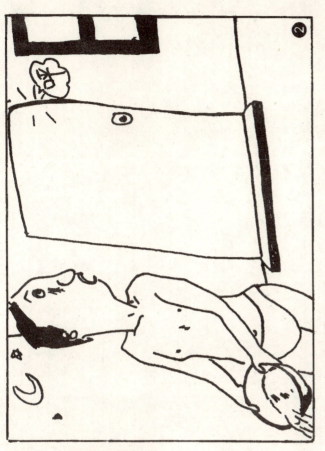

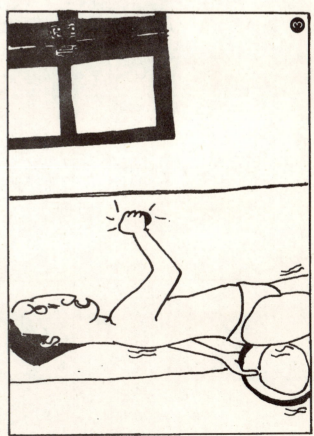

看图说话 4

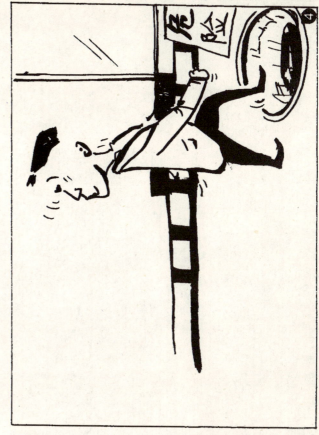

看图说话 5

看图说话 6

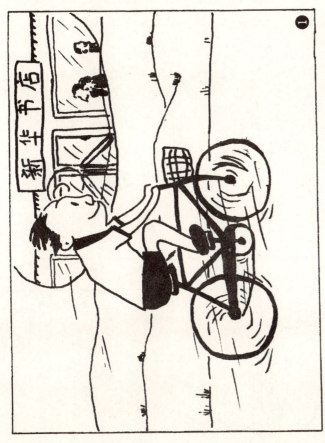

看图说话 7

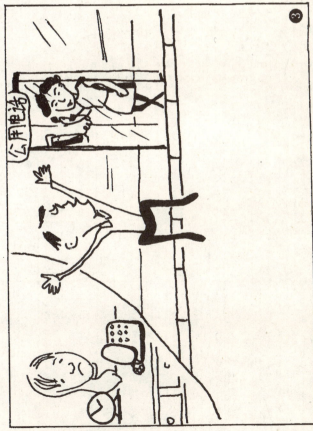

看图说话 8

看图说话 10

看图说话 11

看图说话 13

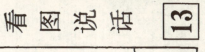
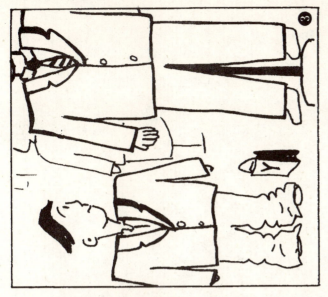

看图说话 14

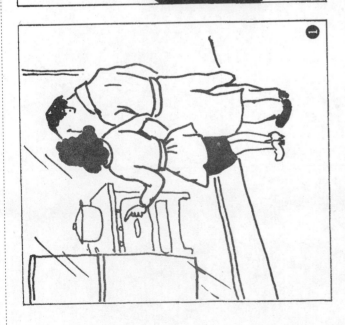
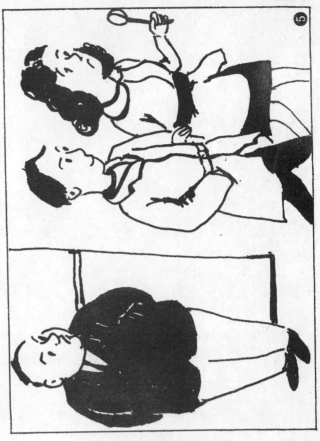

看图说话 15

看图说话 17

看图说话 18

看图说话 19

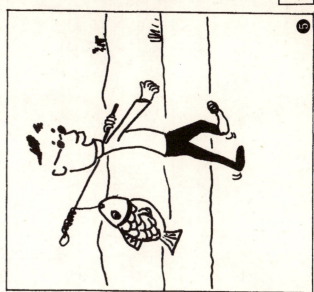
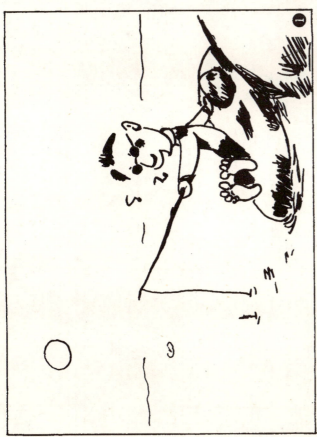

看图说话 20

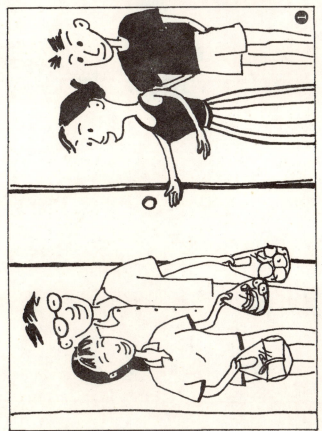

五、看图编故事

练习目的

　　这项练习提供几幅具有连续性情节的画面。要求学生通过讨论,根据画面内容编造一个完整的故事。与前一部分的看图说话不同,这部分练习更强调了练习的刺激性和创造性。虽然图片上的几幅画面的情节也具有连续性,但是又因为其中一幅画面空白,没有提供任何的故事情节,为学生设计了一个自由创造的交际空间,这就要求学生深入细致地讨论。这是个积极的富有创造性的讨论过程。在讨论时学生要充分发挥想像力,根据整套图片所提供的信息,进行合理的推理,共同编造出一个完整的故事。

使用说明

　　将学生分成若干组,每组二至四人。首先给学生几分钟准备时间,请每个组的学生一起讨论画面内容,共同编出一个完整的故事,做好发言的准备。发言的时候,教师可以从每个组选一个代表,也可以让每个组的学生分别描述画面中的一部分内容。

　　在发言结束后,听故事者如果对故事的条理性、情节的合理性产生疑问,可向发言的人提出问题,讲故事者要予以解释和说明。

注意事项

　　教师可以将画面相同的或画面不同的图片发给每个组。两种选择图片的方式,教师可以根据实际情况自由决定(见看图说话的注意事项)。

　　首次做这项练习时,教师应先举例说明练习方法,手举那张为举例而准备的图片,向学生展示,与学生共同讨论画面内容,有条理地编出一个故事,使学生明白此项练习的要求。

　　课堂练习结束后,教师可以给学生布置一个课外作业,将练习变为看图写故事。学生要将写好的故事交给教师,教师批改后再发给学生。这样可以使教师全面了解每个学生的练习情况,也可使听、说、读、写四种技能训练较好地结合,有助于学生全面提高目的语水平。

5. Creating a Story

Purpose:

In this exercise students in small groups are provided with a series of pictures on a single sheet of paper. Through discussion the students create a complete story based on the theme and plot portrayed in the pictures. This is different from the previous *Telling a Story* section in that it requires more creativity and provides more stimulation. This is because, although each of the several small pictures on each page is part of a single connected story, one of the pictures is blank, without any story content. This provides the students with a communicative space within which to freely create, requiring them to discuss more deeply and in detail. This is an active and highly creative discussion process. During discussion the students must use their imaginations, and carry out a logical inference based on the information provided in the surrounding pictures, ultimately creating a complete story.

Procedure:

Separate the students into groups, two to four people per group. After passing out the papers, one per group, have each group of students spend several minutes discussing the contents of the pictures, create a single complete story together, and get ready to present their story to the class. During presentations the instructor can choose to select a single person from each group to speak, or can have each member speak a portion of the story.

After each presentation, if there are any concerns with the logic or orderliness of the story, the listeners can express questions to the speakers, and the speakers will need to try to explain or justify their choices in story creation.

Important Points:

The instructor may choose to either give all the groups the same picture, or give a different picture to each group. The instructor can make a choice of which method to use based on actual needs (see *Telling a Story's Important Points* section for more).

The first time through this exercise the instructor should make an example trial run, using the provided example sheet, to show how the exercise should be carried out. The teacher should hold the example sheet before the class, discuss the content together with the students, and together create a reasonable story. This will help to ensure that students understand the requirements of the exercise.

After the exercise the instructor may set up an out-of-class homework by requiring students to write out a story based on the pictures, to be turned in to the teacher, and later returned to the student. In this way the teacher can better understand each student's progress, and make this exercise into a general unified practice of the four major skills of listening, speaking, reading, and writing, and thus helping to raise the student's overall level in the target language.

看图编故事 举例

看图编故事 **1**

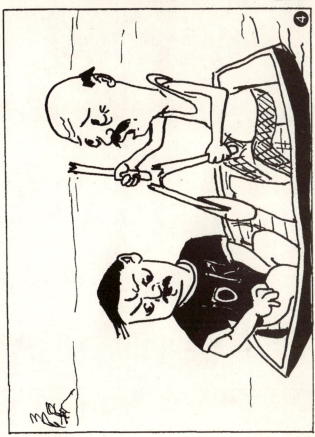

看图编故事 2

看图编故事 3

看图编故事 4

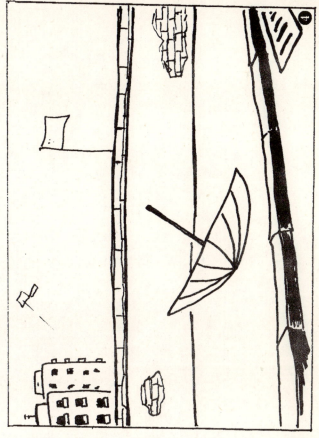

看图编故事 5

看图编故事 6

看图编故事 7

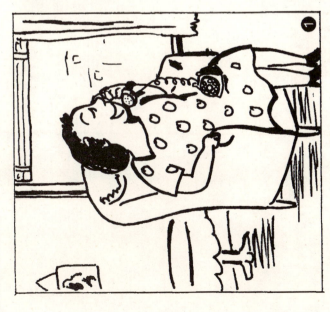

看图编故事 8

看图编故事 9

看图编故事 10

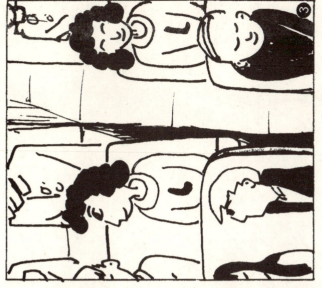

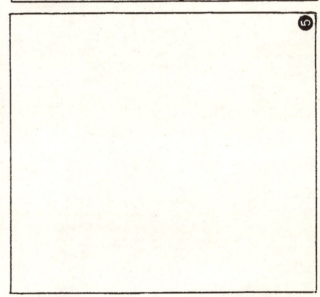

六、看图议论(一)、(二)

练习目的

这项练习提供了揭示现实社会中的某些现象的图片。练习的目的已经由描述、说明转为议论，上升为一种话题性交际，将学生由限制性的交际引向自由表达的新阶段。要求学生能准确、充分、条理清晰地将自己的看法表达出来。练习(一)有1幅画面，更着重于对一个话题的深入讨论；练习(二)有4幅画面，更着重于将话题的广泛性压缩、抽象化。

使用说明

将学生分成若干组，最好每组三人。教师发给每个组一张图片(可以是内容相同的，也可以是内容不同的；如何选择参看"看图说话"部分的注意事项)，给学生10–15分钟的时间，请每个组的学生一起商量讨论，准备发言。

发言分三个步骤，首先应清楚描述画面所提供的内容，然后说明这幅画面所揭示的社会现象，最后发表对这种现象的看法。教师应向学生强调练习的三个步骤，同时板书：1. 描述；2. 说明；3. 议论。此项练习重在议论，因此在论述过程中，要求学生观点明确，论述充分，条理清晰。

发言的方式最好几人分工合作，有人描述，有人说明，有人议论。在准备过程中，几个人应齐心协力，共同商量讨论。

一个组在发言时，别的组学生如果与他们的观点不一致，可以在这个组发言结束后，马上向他们提出问题，展开辩论。这样有助于增强练习的刺激性，活跃课堂气氛，更能使学生在辩论中自然学会一些交际技巧。(比如说，怎样反驳对方，怎样提出异议等等。)

注意事项

首次做这项练习时，教师应先举例说明练习方法，手举那张为举例而准备的图片，向学生展示，按照使用说明所要求的三个步骤依次进行示范。

课堂练习结束后，教师可以给学生布置一个课外作业，将说变为写。学生要将写好的文章交给教师，教师批改后再发给学生。这样可以使教师全面了解每个学生的练习情况，也使听、说、读、写四种技能训练较好地结合，有助于学生全面提高目的语水平。

6. Discussing a Topic I & II

Purpose:

In this exercise students in small groups are provided with a sheet of pictures expressing issues taken from real society. The goal as the students work through the exercise is to go from *description* to *explanation*, and finally to *discussion*, as a form of topical communication, taking the students from a limited communication towards a freer and more expressive new communicative stage. Students need to accurately, fully, and in a clear and well-ordered fashion express their opinions. Type I has one picture per page, and emphasizes thorough discussion of one topic; type II has four pictures per page, and emphasizes generalization and abstraction.

Procedure:

Separate the students into groups, optimally with three people per group. Provide one sheet per group (each group can have identical, or different sheets, based on teacher preference; see *Important Points* section for *Telling a Story* for more information), and give the students 10 – 15 minutes to discuss and prepare to present.

Presentation has three steps. First the students should clearly describe the picture contents. Then they should explain what social issue is represented in the picture. Finally, they should express their opinion towards that issue. The instructor should emphasize these steps with the students, and can write out the steps "1) describe; 2) explain; 3) discuss" on the board. Since the emphasis of this exercise is group discussion, students are required to come up with a clear point of view, discuss it fully, and express it clearly.

Presentations are best given as a group, each person taking a part, with one person describing, one explaining, and one discussing. During preparation the members should work together closely, and discuss the issue as a group.

Immediately after a group has presented, other groups can ask questions if they do not agree, or express other opinions. This makes the exercise more stimulating and enlivens the classroom environment, helping the students to naturally learn some communicative techniques (for example, how to oppose someone, how to express different views, etc.).

Important Points:

The first time through this exercise the instructor should go through an example trial run, using the provided example sheet to show how the exercise should be carried out. The teacher should hold the example sheet before the class, and walk through each of the three steps.

After the exercise the instructor may set up an out-of-class homework by requiring students to write out a story based on the pictures, to be turned in to the teacher, and later returned to the student. In this way the teacher can better understand each student's progress, and make this exercise into a general unified practice of the four major skills of listening, speaking, reading, and writing, and thus helping to raise the student's overall level in the target language.

看图议论 举例

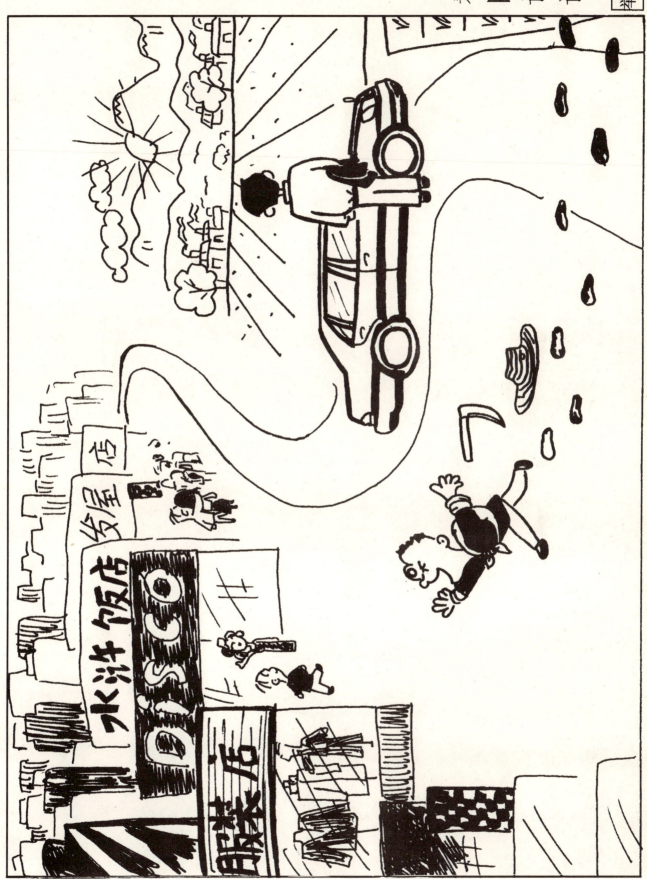

看图议论 （一） 1、2

看图议论　　（一）　3、4

看图议论　（一）　5、6

看图议论 （二）

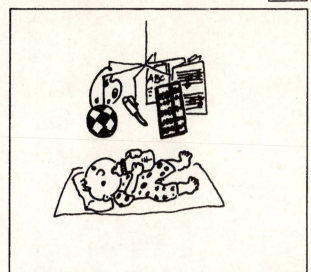

看图议论 （二） 2

看图议论 （二） 3

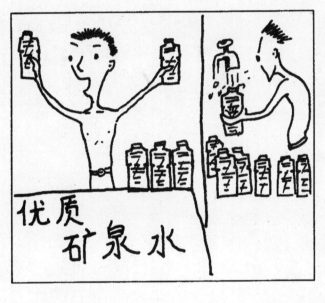

看图议论 （二） 4

看图议论 （二） 5

看图议论 （二） 6

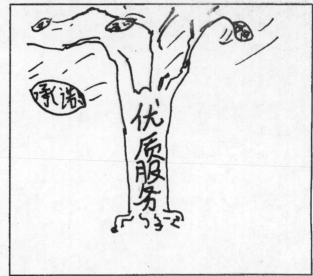

后　记

目前世界第二语言教学越来越重视提高学生的语言交际能力。交际法成为广为流行的教学思想。同时，语言教师越来越认识到课堂练习方式的多样化有助于活跃课堂气氛，提高课堂教学的效率。然而在这方面至今比较缺少较为系统的、供课堂交际练习所使用的教材。

近些年来，很多教师都在摸索尝试一些有益的方法。我们从中受到很大启发，并且根据我们的实际教学经验，也创造了一些新的练习方式。

我们从1996年12月动手编写此书，在一年多的时间里，在编写及试用过程中，得到了中央民族大学汉语中心、外语系、干训部以及美国俄勒冈大学诸多教师的大力支持，在此谨向他们致以诚挚的谢意。本书的出版同样凝结着北京语言文化大学出版社的领导以及责任编辑陈华兰老师的心血，对于他们所给予的帮助和付出的劳动谨致谢忱！

由于本书是一本探索中的书，不足之处，在所难免，欢迎各位同仁专家批评指正。

卢百可　　邓秀均　　宁卓涛
1998年8月于北京

作者简介

卢百可（Patrick Lucas），1996年毕业于美国俄勒冈大学（University of Oregon）语言学系应用语言学专业，获硕士学位。1996年8月至1998年6月任美国俄勒冈州高教系统驻京代表。

邓秀均，1991年6月毕业于中央民族大学民语二系维吾尔语言文学专业，获学士学位，毕业后留校从事对外汉语教学工作，现为中央民族大学对外汉语中心讲师。

宁卓涛，1997年6月毕业于中央民族大学美术系油画专业。

Postscript

As more and more importance is attached to communicative competence in second language teaching and learning, the communicative method of language teaching is widely applied in second language classrooms. Meanwhile, more and more teachers have realized that diversified exercises in the classroom help create an atmosphere favorable for efficient language learning. Yet there are not very many textbooks available so far to provide systematic communicative exercises for classroom practices.

In recent years, efforts have been made by many teachers in an attempt to meet this need. Enlightened by their ideas and based on our own teaching experience, we have designed some new forms of exercises of our own, many of which are included in the present book.

The compilation of this book started in December 1996. We would like to express our thanks to the teachers at the Chinese Language Department, the Foreign Languages Department and the Cadre – Training Department of the Central University for Nationalities, and the teachers at the University of Oregon, for their support in the compilation and trial of the book. Our thanks also goes to Ms Chen Hualan and the Beijing Language and Culture University Press for their work and effort in the publication of the book.

Patrick Lucas
Deng Xiujun
Ning Zhuotao
Beijing, August 1998

Authors

Patrick Lucas, graduated with M.A. from the Department of Linguistics of the University of Oregon in 1996, and worked in Beijing(August 1996 – June 1998) as a representative of the Department of Higher Education of the State of Oregon.

Deng Xiujun, graduated in 1996 from the Department of Minority Languages of the Central University for Nationalities, and has been teaching Chinese at the University since graduation.

Ning Zhuotao, graduated from the Fine Arts Department of the Central University for Nationalities in 1997.

27